Memory and Honor

Memory and Honor

Cultural and Generational Ministry
with Korean American Communities

Simon C. Kim

Forewords by
Virgilio Elizondo and
Peter C. Phan

A Michael Glazier Book

LITURGICAL PRESS
Collegeville, Minnesota

www.litpress.org

A Michael Glazier Book published by Liturgical Press

Cover design by Ann Blattner.
Cover image by Dorin Hwang. Used by permission.

1   2   3   4   5   6   7   8   9

Library of Congress Cataloging-in-Publication Data

Kim, Simon C.
   Memory and honor : cultural and generational ministry with Korean American communities / Simon C. Kim.
      pages   cm
   "A Michael Glazier book."
   Includes bibliographical references.
   ISBN 978-0-8146-8215-9 — ISBN 978-0-8146-8240-1 (e-book)
   1. Church work with Korean Americans.   I. Title.

BV4468.2.K6K57   2013
282.089'957073—dc23   2012048189

Contents

Foreword

The church of today has gone far beyond past understandings of what it means to be church. Many writings and even church members presuppose a uniformity of language, customs, tradition, and heritage. The reality today is becoming something quite different and much more complex.

Migrations today are taking place faster than ever before. The United States, as can be said of Europe and the American continent, is becoming a rich encounter of all the peoples of the world. It is a very interesting dynamic how as migrants come in, they both change the culture of the country while at the same time being changed by it. They maintain some of their original identity while at the same time assuming many of the elements of the host country. This is not an easy process, but it takes place in many different ways and at a pace that cannot be determined by anyone. Gradually, a new identity emerges in continuity with the past yet a stranger to it, biologically rooted in the homeland yet culturally growing in a new space, identifying with the present yet projecting into the future.

What does all this movement of peoples mean for the church in the United States? The church was born as a church of immigrants and gradually nursed them into becoming the church of the U.S. As new immigrants come in, they will be gradually incorporated into the church while contributing the various gifts of their own tradition. The unity of our church in the U.S. is not the unity of a single instrument but that of a symphony of many instruments, a chorus of many voices, a tapestry of many colors.

The U.S. Catholic Church has become very aware of the contributions and challenges of the black church with its painful memory of slavery and rich heritage of liberating gospel hymns. It is also recognizing the contributions of the Latino church with its painful memory of conquest, the dynamic process of *mestizaje* and the very colorful and popular religious traditions. But there are other elements of the rich encounter that still need to be recognized. Some have been here a long time and others are only more recently arriving. Regardless of when they arrived, they are adding to the richness and complexity of our church: one church with many languages, customs and traditions—a remarkable expression of our catholicity!

Korean Americans are a very important element of the American Catholic experience. Father Simon Kim is making a great contribution not just to the Korean American people but also to the church of the U.S. First of all, he is helping Korean Americans to assume their history and appreciate themselves as they are today. It is marvelous to interact with our Korean American students at Notre Dame and learn about their experiences of feeling alienated at times and welcomed at others, sometimes distant from their own elders and other times open to learning from the wisdom of their elders. Young people are Korean but not just Korean because they are also American! They are becoming something new and the challenge is to retain the very best of their Korean families and heritage as they forge their lives in the U.S.

This book will also help the church to recognize, value, and welcome Korean American Catholics not by asking them to cease being who they are and become "American" but simply accepting them as they are. Cultural values, family loyalty, a deep sense of honor, and many other attributes of Korean American Catholics are presented in this book and are one of its most important contributions.

Memory and Honor is not simply a description of Korean immigrants and Korean Americans today but rather a reflection on the heritage of departure, displacement, and resettlement as the key of identity and hope for those continuing to live in between two cultures, languages, and belief systems of Korea and the U.S. Life in the "in between" is like the birth of a child who receives some of the features from the mother and some from the father but in the end is truly a new creation. As a U.S. Latino, I can truly appreciate this as I am a *mestizo*—a child of Mexico and the U.S.

On a very personal note, I have enjoyed and learned very much working with Father Simon Kim—very Korean and very American. He is a true example of what he is speaking about throughout this book. All of us in the church and society owe him a tremendous debt of gratitude for this pioneering, enlightening, and very enjoyable book.

Virgilio Elizondo
Professor of Pastoral and Hispanic Theology
University of Notre Dame

A book on Korean American Catholics is long overdue, and no one is more qualified to write it than Simon C. Kim, himself a Korean American priest, with recognized expertise on contextual theology and extensive pastoral experience with migrant communities.

It is an open secret that Asian American Catholics, the majority of whom are Filipino, Vietnamese, and Korean, together with Latino/a Catholics, will make up the majority of the American Catholic Church within a couple of decades. Yet white American Catholics know precious little about them and their types of Catholicism and not much has been done at the institutional and organizational levels to prepare the American Catholic Church for this demographic shift.

We are deeply grateful to Simon Kim for introducing us to Korean American Catholics, the history of their Catholicism back in Korea, their beginnings as migrants in this country, and their situation of social, cultural, and religious displacement and in-betweenness. This minority condition of Korean American Catholics, "a minority of minorities," in Kim's memorable phrase, is, however, not simply a disadvantage to overcome but also an opportunity to live a new way of being a Christian. It reminds the American Catholic Church, which is still the largest and even the most powerful Christian denomination in the U.S., of God's self-emptying or kenotic mode of acting among us, as weakness and not as power.

Kim's book is felicitously titled *Memory and Honor*. Asian American Catholics should *remember* their roots, even as they try to be incorporated into the larger American church. And they should *honor* those who have remained in their native countries and those who have come to the U.S. before them. Dwelling in the interstices between the two shores, American Asian Christians, Catholics as well as Protestants and Evangelicals, are called to join hands to witness to God's presence among us. We are thankful to Kim for having shown us the way.

Peter C. Phan
The Ignacio Ellacuría Chair of Catholic
   Social Thought
Georgetown University

Preface

At a recent conference in North Carolina, a Korean American young adult, who works for one of the Senators in Washington, D.C., described the Korean reality as "crabs trapped in a bucket." This was an unusual metaphor to describe the reality of this particular immigrant group—a metaphor I had never heard before. As he began to liken Korean Americans to these crustaceans, the reality of the Korean American psyche, attitudes, and conditions became vividly clear to the audience. "Crabs trapped in a bucket" struggle at all costs to survive. They claw and crawl their way over each other in the hope that their individual efforts will bring release. These crabs caught in a bucket compete with one another to climb their way to the top. They grab the lead crab on top and drag it down in the hopes of rising to the top themselves. This repeated struggle becomes a futile cycle as no progress is made. Rather than a few rising to the top with the help of those below, the instinctive temptation of the many on the bottom to bring down others is too great.

Comparing the people of Korean descent residing in the U.S. to "crabs trapped in a bucket" seems like harsh criticism, but this metaphor does contain several elements of truth. The rationale for the "crabs in a bucket" mentality can be attributed to communal events in the history of the Korean and Korean American people—traumatic events such as foreign occupation of their homeland, wars, poverty, and the immigrant experience of departure, displacement, and resettlement in a new land. What makes Korean immigrants and their offspring unique is the generational transmission of this condition, referred to as *han*. Being "crabs trapped in the bucket," unconsciously and instinctually not allowing others to succeed, is a Korean way of life. The irony is that Koreans are a communal ethnic group. The individual accomplishments needed for such a cultural celebration are, however, often denigrated.

Writing a book such as *Memory and Honor: Cultural and Generational Ministry with Korean American Communities* has placed me right in the middle of the bucket. There will be some who applaud my theological reflections on the immigration experience and especially on a religious group that has not been heard from to any significant extent. Others will read my reflections on Korean immigrants and their offspring and find that it does not resonate with their reality. Finally, there will be those who want to bring down my effort because of their natural instinct to do so. A *kairos* (birthing) moment is upon us, however, since the consciousness of the immigrant reality and especially the next generation is maturing, and both church and society are ready for such a conversation to begin.

I am certainly not presuming that my theological reflection is the definitive word on the immigrant experience of Koreans in the U.S., nor that it is the complete summation of the Korean Catholic faith life of the U.S. Catholic Church. Rather, *Memory and Honor* is my humble attempt to give voice to the voiceless and to the minority of minorities. By giving voice to the immigrant generation, I want to acknowledge their courage in bringing their families to a foreign land for greater opportunities in all facets of life. By giving voice to Korean American Catholics, I hope to raise the awareness of the next generation's situation in life and to encourage those reading these pages, especially Korean Americans themselves, to reflect on their unique reality. These pages begin the conversation that is so needed in our modern, pluralistic society, both within my culture and religious community and in society as a whole, regardless of culture, race, or creed.

Living within two cultures, two worlds, is difficult enough. Reflecting on and then writing about both realities are truly a challenge. Linguistic and cultural nuances of the immigration experience make communication difficult, because categories are not always compatible or coherent. Even the basic terminology of what to call the people of Korean descent in the U.S. is problematic. There is no Korean word for "Korean Americans" other than a generic listing of the generations as immigrants. In addition, the original immigrants always refer to themselves as Korean and never acknowledge their hyphenated status as Korean Americans. The next generation speaks of themselves interchangeably as both Korean and Korean American, blurring the distinction between the two worlds. As the history of Koreans living in the U.S. continues, trying to identify one's category becomes even more difficult. At the same conference in North Carolina, another Korean American young adult presented his five possible categories of this ethnic group: Korean Koreans, Koreans, Korean Americans, American Koreans, and Americans were all labels that he and his peers used for others who appear similar to them and for their own reality as well. In short, the description of any ethnic group faces this dilemma. This was also my experience with *Memory and Honor*. The lack of appropriate terminology in the Korean language for people living in the U.S., along with the confusing delineations between generations by Korean Americans, is evident throughout this book. Trying to address Koreans within the immigrant generation and the next was truly a complicated and conscientious endeavor. The more I focused on such distinctions, the more I realized the privilege and burden of my own reality. The privilege is that I am able to engage both Korean and Korean American realities; the burden is that more and more I am also caught between these two worlds.

My being also is a non-being. Having lived most of my life in the U.S. (over forty years), my Korean features do not qualify me to be considered Korean by those in Korea, and my "accent-less" English does not qualify me as an American by those in the U.S. At times, it is strange to be in a group of Korean priests and not be considered one of them. "He's not a Korean priest," they say in Korean and introduce me as something other. While serving in English-speaking parishes, I have often experienced people coming up to me at the end of Mass and commenting how pleased they were because they could understand me since I spoke without an accent. To add to the confusion, even though I came to the United States at a very young age, I am not considered first generation because I was born in Korea. Neither am I considered 1.5 generation nor second generation because my immigration story began at two years of age. Thus, my being is a nonbeing. Nevertheless, being in the middle of cultures, languages, generations, or even countries is not necessarily negative. I have been fortunate to be able to navigate from one world to the other and glean from both cultures. Although others with similar immigration stories are not always capable of this mobility, all experience the "in betweenness," the being caught at the fringes of two worlds; thus, all share, knowingly or unknowingly, the issues of being Korean American.

The difficulties of subsequent generations of Korean Americans, or any immigrant group for that matter, are not limited just to culture and language. Perhaps a much bigger issue is purpose. The parent generation came to the U.S. with a clear purpose of survival in terms of the social and economic betterment for their families. These values and goals are not, however, easily translated to subsequent generations. Simply surviving is not enough because the next generation has resources and access to society that was not previously available. Therefore, today's challenge is to translate the values and goals of the immigrant generation so subsequent generations can find their identity in society while not losing a heritage beyond the immediate.

Rather than a disadvantage, my nonbeing offers many possibilities not always recognized. Nevertheless, the meaning of our existence, our identity, is ultimately discovered only through service. This, then, is the purpose of Korean Americans, the Korean American promise. Unlike the parent group who had to survive by taking what was offered, Korean Americans are now in a position to give back to their community, the church, and the world. Only by being committed to making these contributions can Korean Americans truly make the U.S. their own because of the commitments made. The very lack of identity, a nonbeing, affords great opportunities because of the view of reality from many different perspectives. Perhaps this passion of mine—the search for who I am within a social, political, and religious context—will spark a fire in others to reflect on what it means to be a people living in between two worlds: people of Korean descent living in America, but not "crabs trapped in a bucket."

Introduction

Why a book on Korean immigrants and Korean Americans? After all, only two historical events mark the presence of Korean immigrants in recent U.S. history. More precisely, two very tragic events stand out for Korean immigrants and Korean Americans when recalling the last four decades of immigration and resettlement in this country. In 1992, the Korean community in the Los Angeles region suffered unfathomable psychological, emotional, and physical damages as the L.A. riots erupted in their surroundings. Fifteen years later in 2007, a Korean American young adult took the lives of thirty-two college students as well as his own at Virginia Tech. The next chapter will further examine these two events, which unknowingly perpetuated the past influences of the Korean heritage upon the immigrant people while at the same time affirming certain characteristics of newly developing Korean Americans. The former tragedy did not distinguish Koreans in the homeland and those living abroad while the latter allowed for the realization of two distinct groups of Koreans and Korean Americans. These two events also reveal the resilience of Korean immigrants and the Korean American people and the potential of the Korean American promise, a gift not only to Korean Americans themselves but also for Koreans in Korea as a way of dealing with the historical and cultural reality of *han*. *Memory and Honor: Cultural and Generational Ministry with Korean American Communities* is an examination of how the U.S. experience provides the people of Korean descent a unique opportunity to reevaluate and re-create the values and goals of life through the immigration process. As Korea rises in political, social, and economic status around the world and the U.S. continues its influential presence in a global society, Korean Americans are capable of reaping the richness of both their country of origin and their country of destination today.

It is only appropriate that we are reminded of these two tragedies today at the same time as we observe the twentieth anniversary of the

Los Angeles riots (1992) and the fifth anniversary of the Virginia Tech shooting (2007). Tragedies on the west and east coasts of the U.S. indiscriminatingly impacted the immigrant generation and their offspring—but in vastly different ways. Both occasions contribute to the burdens of a people known by their unique hardship in life often referred to as *han*. *Han* is an inexpressible reality due to a unique and common historical-cultural experience and understanding of the Korean people. As descendants of this unique people from the Far East, the Korean diaspora in the U.S. provides fertile soil for the continuation and further negative growth of *han*. At the same time, the U.S. also provides Korean Americans a positive opportunity for embracing *han* by their privileged position in between two very rich cultural worlds of Korea and the U.S. Thus, *Memory and Honor* is not simply a description of Korean immigrants and Korean Americans today but rather an examination of our heritage that should not be discounted or taken for granted. It is a task, a calling for proper reflection on Korean Americans—one that is best done by Korean Americans and not by outsiders—for the potential significance it has for future generations living in the U.S. as well as to all Koreans everywhere as a "way" of embracing and releasing *han*.

These tragedies are so significant that they have left an indelible mark on a whole cultural group within generations. For many Korean Americans as well as the rest of the U.S., the significance of these events has not been fully realized, and the real impact of such a history on a specific ethnic group starting with the immigrant generation and then trickling to the next has been vastly overlooked. At first glance, one can simply surmise negative results from such events, especially in light of the psychological, emotional, and physical damages as witnessed in the destruction of property and human life. However, these tragedies also reveal the resilience of the Korean people and how such powerful characteristics are being transformed in Korean Americans today. Rather than overlooking tragedies, as is often the case with Confucian cultures since the embarrassment of such events bring "dishonor," Korean Americans must now do the work of remembering so that the endured hardships can be truly appreciated by their own community as well as by the rest of this country of immigrants.

Korean Americans who are now coming into their own as well as having something positive to offer the rest of society can do so only by recognizing their unique past. With ongoing immigration, Korean Americans must properly reflect on their own situation, especially as a generation caught in between cultures and generations to assist others coming afterward with both identity and hope. *Memory and Honor* examines both the immigrant generation as well as their offspring in the experiences of rupture, displacement, and resettlement as the key to identity and hope for those continuing to live in between the two cultures, languages, and belief systems of Korea and the U.S.

Why a book on Korean American Catholicism? After all, displacement caused by the immigration process is usually followed by resettlement in the host country where the ideals of dominant society tend to overshadow one's personal heritage. Depending on the politically correct term of the day, immigrants are supposed to assimilate, acculturate, or merge into every aspect of mainstream society, including the church. Korean immigrants in the U.S. are expected to resettle by learning English and becoming a regular part of church and society. Remembering their customs and rituals is acceptable, but Asian immigrants are expected to be "American" while maintaining their heritage from a distance and when appropriate. Their counterpart in U.S. history, the European immigrants, went through a similar process of departure from their original homelands, displacement as minorities, only to resettle in the U.S. as part of a "homogeneous" religious and cultural group, and recognize their heritage mostly in festive celebrations, foods, and other cultural images today. Part of their "success" in staking their claim in a new land resulted because of their similarities: a learned common language; similar appearance to one another because of their fair skin; and social acceptance, especially in marriage. Thus, their success in resettling stems from their abilities to become part of a homogeneous religious and cultural group while acknowledging the contributions of their European heritage without it being a barrier to one another, as was previously the case. The U.S. Catholic Church underwent a similar transition as the once heavily influenced European immigrant church divided by her Irish, Italian, Polish, and German roots followed a similar pattern of merging into a singular U.S. Catholic enclave. The adjustment linguistically, socially, and culturally of the early European immigrant groups thus became the "model" of the immigration experience upheld for generations to come. So the question still remains, why do we need a book on Catholicism focusing specifically on one ethnic group in the U.S. when the initial U.S. social and ecclesial experience has been one of similarities rather than divisions along ethnic lines?

The answer to this question is beginning to emerge in church and society beyond people of Korean descent. Unlike previous immigrants to the U.S. and their subsequent generations, Asian Americans are not able to repeat a similar process or pattern of immigration of the early twentieth century because they will always appear foreign regardless of their generational longevity. The similarities among European immigrant groups that allowed them to become a singular unit in society cannot be replicated by Asian immigrants since it is biological. Neither the duration of time in the U.S. nor the level of English proficiency is enough to imitate the success European immigrants had in resettlement. The barriers that kept Europeans initially apart in their immigration experience dissolved into a reminiscent memory, no longer threatening to church or society. Immigrants from Asia continually live with the barriers that do not subside into the background but are perpetuated as distinctions from Euro-Americans.

Another factor why Asian Americans are not able to achieve the levels of their predecessors is based on the surroundings encountered upon resettlement. The U.S. is not a new frontier as it was when the European settlers first came. Rather, there are complex structures and regulations already in place that are not always accommodating. For European immigrants, being the "first" migrants in an environment raw with resources and possibilities meant they had plenty of opportunities to forge new communities, political and social networks, and ecclesial structures. By doing so prior to any social, political, or religious establishment, European immigrants created their own space, which gave them ownership of this country. However, later immigrants, such as the Asian population, followed after structures were firmly in place; thus, these migrants were expected to conform to the current establishment rather than take full ownership in their new environment. A result of this is the way faith journeys of Korean immigrants and subsequent generations are not considered as authentic expressions of church until full integration occurs. Like all Asian religious groups, this minority community is expected to integrate into English-speaking parishes as well as the current political and social networks. This view is held not only by dominant members in society but also by Korean Americans themselves as they struggle, at times, with an inferior sense of self. However, if Asian immigrants are seen as an asset affording significant contributions to both church and society, then local communities such as Korean Americans would be better appreciated and allowed to develop in their unique immigrant history as a way of birthing something new for all of society.

The U.S. has been called the land of immigrants. What makes church and society healthy and unique in the U.S. has been the influx and influence of immigrants throughout its history. To continue this tradition of not only receiving immigrants as one of its social and ecclesial members, the U.S. must continue to learn, respect, and cultivate the ethnic and religious differences that make this country unique. Thus, *Memory and Honor* is to give voice to the first generation of immigrants, the first ones to experience their minority status, and their offspring who become the minority of minorities, Korean American Catholics, who are an ethnic minority as well as a religious minority since a majority of Korean immigrants are Protestants. Even the least among us has a great contribution to make if we take the Scripture to heart (Luke 9:48). As a minority group and as a minority of minorities, Korean American Catholics may have more to contribute to church and society since this country and faith have been founded, developed, and maintained by immigrants such as these. To better appreciate Korean American Catholic contributions and to truly see this ethnic immigrant community as an authentic expression of church, the immigration history must first be examined. Without knowing how Korean American Catholics became a hyphenated reality, their worth to church and society will never be realized.

Korean immigration at the turn of the twentieth century did not capture enough national attention to merit such dialogue regarding their contributions. Many Korean immigrants of this era came not to make a new home for themselves but for political and economic reasons. Not until the final decades of the century did Korean immigrants and their offspring become aware of their position in society, warranting such discussions as an ethnic contribution to church and society. Prior to this revelation, Asian immigrant groups such as Korean Americans were seen as "model minorities" working diligently to obtain the "American Dream" rather than contributing to the transformation of church and society. Today, society is in flux between seeing Asian Americans as true contributors rather than just "model participants," especially in ecclesial settings. However, discussions of this nature are beginning to surface because internal and external factors throughout the world are challenging the U.S. and the Catholic Church's way of being. As stated previously, what made this country unique and the Catholic Church a social presence were the immigrants of their day. This reality still rings true today as the degree to which we embrace immigrants in our midst reveals the character of our church and society. Korean Americans, like any immigrant group, are able to make an invaluable contribution in every aspect of their lives. Thus, a study of Korean American Catholicism can shed light on how to be church in relation to the everyday concerns of society, especially as migration increases globally. *Memory and Honor* not only serves the Korean American communities but, more importantly, allows the rest of society to understand the societal and ecclesial gifts from the immigrant communities and their offspring.

A cultural and generational divide has developed over time with Koreans and Korean Americans, as evident during my visits to Korea and personal encounters here in the U.S. When I was in my twenties, my visits to Korea always included the older generation's insistence that I was very Korean even though I struggled with the language. No matter how differently I acted or spoke in broken Korean, I was still accepted as one of them. During these trips, I was always reminded I was Korean, especially in their farewell blessings upon my return. Over a decade later, even though my Korean language proficiency increased and my understanding of some of the cultural phenomena surpassed those of even my parents' group, I am not considered a Korean when in the midst of my Korean peers. I recall moments when these distinctions were pointed out when being introduced for the first time. Comments were made that distinguished who I was as a non-Korean from the Koreans from Korea in group settings. For example, during my doctoral studies in Washington, D.C., some of the Korean priests there as foreign students would introduce me as a non-Korean, trying to make a distinction from their reality and further confusing my own background. What made this increasingly more uncomfortable is the lack of wording for Korean Americans like myself in the Korean language. Yes, there are terms for immigrants living in the U.S. or Koreans in the diaspora, but no terminology accounting for my current status in life as a Korean American with a hyphenated reality. Thus, such introductions attempting to delineate Koreans from Korean Americans actually meant that I was neither a Korean nor an American. Even with the certitude of who I am as a person with a hyphenated identity, their distinction still left a sour taste in my mouth.

As immigrants, Korean Americans have a slightly different history from their counterparts back home. The events surrounding the Korean War and the poverty in its aftermath are the last common ground. Once Koreans left their homeland, they began a new chapter of their lives, intersecting, but never quite the same as those found in their homelands. This departure and life in the Korean diaspora is often differentiated from the homeland and referred to in Korean by the difference in waters found in local wells. Drinking from different wells than those in the homeland produces different characteristics according to the Korean mind-set; however, more importantly, this proverbial saying further highlights the overall unique situation of the Korean American people. The waters in the well have changed not only because of distance but also generationally in each locale. A good example of this is the Korean immigration experience of the seventies and eighties compared with those of recent immigrants. Four decades ago, Koreans underwent experiences of rupture, displacement, and resettlement that made them distinct from their counterparts in Korea as well as immigrants today who come with more resources and education. The unique beginnings of the Korean encounter on U.S. soil provide the foundation for the positive contribution previously mentioned, the capability to embrace and release *han* in the lives of all ethnic Koreans as well as the wider society. Today's task is to uncover the events leading up to displacement and resettlement, delineate similarities and differences between the lives of Koreans and Korean Americans, and, most importantly, promulgate the significance and contribution Korean Americans are able to make to overall society because of this hyphenated reality, a perspective that is not available to all.

Part of understanding this hyphenated reality begins by understanding people's historical beginnings back in their native lands. The other aspect, perhaps more important than the first, is the comprehension of the reasons for leaving one's native land and beginning a historic journey that distinguishes immigrants from their counterparts back home. Although stories have been pieced together to create a historical narrative, the legacy of this narrative has not been realized. The unspoken purpose of immigration among the Korean communities is beginning to create a chasm, not only between natives and immigrants, but also generationally in the U.S. as their lack of immigrant history contributes to the lack of identity. Original reasons based on economic or political stability can no longer be the sole claim for immigration since the standard of living in Korea has increased drastically. In many circumstances, Korean immigrants, working in less prestigious jobs, are now living below the income levels of their Korean counterparts. In fact, a recent study revealed how Korean Americans also have not attained similar income levels of other Asian immigrant groups:

> [T]he income earned by Korean Americans is less than that of other Asian American groups (U.S. Census Bureau, 2007). For example, in 2004, the median household income for all Asian American groups was $56,161, and the median household income for Korean Americans was $43,195 (U.S. Census Bureau, 2007). Korean American households earned 23% less than did all Asian American households and 3% less than did all U.S. households (U.S. Census Bureau, 2007).

Furthermore, Korean Americans choose college majors resulting in starting salaries that are significantly lower than those of majors typically chosen by other Asian American groups.[1]

Financial instability devalues the immigration process for many Korean Americans seeking a better life. Most immigrants seldom have measures of their success when resettling in an unfamiliar environment other than monetary worth. Thus, financial gain becomes the overwhelming indicator of whether an individual or group validates the reason for immigration. However, when the opposite occurs, the devaluation of resources and wealth, self-esteem is lowered, causing a gap not only between Korean immigrants and those in Korea but also among individuals within the Korean American communities. Whether distinctions are made by external sources, such as government agencies, or internal sources through the lessening of self-worth by the lack of monetary gains, Korean Americans are straddled with a self-consciousness that marginalizes them from mainstream American society as well as their Korean heritage.

Another problem that leads to much confusion is the label "Korean Americans." This is a vague description that has not been clearly defined. Because of the unique history of immigration rallying the people of Korean descent in the U.S., the time has come for Korean Americans to accept their reality as different yet familiar to their counterparts across the Pacific. Through the impact of the U.S. culture—the drinking from different wells—the transformation of a people has occurred. Thus, with an acceptance as a hyphenated people, a healthy embrace of a Korean American social consciousness can be realized.

Once the waters from the different wells have been tasted, there is no going back to what was before. Therefore, a true appreciation of what makes Korean Americans different is vital for one's identity and appropriate societal and ecclesial response. A positive social consciousness is necessary to properly address Korean Americans in their distinctive situation in life and not simply as offshoots of real Koreans. This will bring about a "second-class citizen" mentality. For example, rather than applying ready-made religious prescriptions found in Korea, Korean Americans are in need of pathways accounting for their different presence in the U.S. as

---

[1] Kevin Kelly, Ae-jung Chang Gunsalus, and Robert Gunsalus, "Social Cognitive Predictors of the Career Goals of Korean American Students," *The Career Development Quarterly* 58 (2009): 16.

Korean descendants. In other words, what works in the country of origin and the host country may be useful and successful, but they must also be incorporated into something new and practical for Korean Americans.

Often, the separation of Koreans and Korean Americans has a negative connotation. Part of this can be attributed to the fact Koreans overly protect their "Koreanness" out of survival instincts due to historical domination and oppression. Thus, being other than or diluting one's "Koreanness" has been historically looked down upon. One example fueling this separation is found in the "condescending and patronizing attitudes" of *gyo pos*, a Korean term designating those who have emigrated from Korea, as many felt betrayed at the departure of some of their own friends and family.[2] "Korean Americans are depicted as rejecting any community with South Korean nationals (or even fellow Korean immigrants), in favor of making money."[3]

Another example of this mind-set is evident with the racially mixed children of the Korean War as American servicemen married impoverished Korean women. Not only were the Korean women labeled as prostitutes for marrying outside their own culture, but their children faced further discrimination as they were labeled *tui-gi*, a derogatory term derived from inanimate objects. The disdain for any aberrations of "Koreanness" has in many ways contributed to limiting a Korean American social consciousness. Rather than embracing the richness of both heritages of the East and the West, Korean Americans have been stunted in their growth as a unique people with valuable contributions to both church and society.

The purpose of *Memory and Honor* is to raise the awareness of a Korean American social consciousness, especially in its Catholic character, a catholicity that is eschatological in nature, for it is where we are headed while being already upon us but not fully realized. By examining from the beginning some personal reasons for immigration rather than generic statements relating to the attainment of a better life, Korean Americans can acknowledge and discover rich characteristics of their heritage of both worlds that make them who they are today. Only in the discovery of one's identity can a Korean American Catholic heritage also be realized, for the spiritual is always in relation to all the other areas of our lives.

---

[2] Min-Jung Kim, "Moments of Danger in the (Dis)continuous Relation of Korean Nationalism and Korean American Nationalism," *Positions* 5, no. 2 (1997): 370.

[3] Ibid., 369.

The Korean Immigrant Catholic Churches

With the rapid economic rise of Korea within the last few decades, the church in Korea has also increased dramatically. The Korean Catholic Church has gone from a history of receiving missioners to become one herself, as several Korean religious men and women are now serving in various parts of the world. Here in the U.S., the Korean Catholic communities have been so-called mission territory since its inception. Many Korean priests, some foreign missioners who served in Korea, such as the Maryknoll and Columbans, and few non-Korean-speaking clergy originally founded several of the communities throughout the U.S. Very rarely and only recently do we find faith communities of Korean heritage founded by clergy ordained in the U.S. In addition, many of these communities are not recognized as parishes and have the dubious distinction of remaining Korean centers or missions of an English-speaking parish. The arbitrary history of the Korean immigrant Catholic communities still largely staffed today by missioners, religious priests and sisters from Korea, as well as being labeled something other than actual parishes, suppress the necessary and healthy development as a U.S. immigrant and ethnic church, thus stifling any contribution to the universal church in her own way of being an authentic expression of church. Given the rich history of the Catholic Church in Korea and the ongoing presence of the Korean missioners around the world, Korean immigrants and Korean American Catholics are also able to realize a similar gift to their own people and to overall society.

Undoubtedly, the lack of social presence and contribution in mainstream society is also reflected in the ecclesial setting. The Korean Catholic Churches in the U.S. have yet to contribute significantly to others, for they still operate in an inferior mode by simply accepting what others have to offer while not recognizing any of the gifts this hyphenated community is to both the universal church and society. This direct relationship between social presence and contribution in the religious sphere makes today's Korean American Catholic task both holistic and universal. Simply following the lead of the Catholic Church in Korea and the society oversees does not make any more sense than for Korean immigrants and their offspring to simply follow the ways of the U.S. Catholic Church and mainstream society. Being of two heritages requires an incorporation of the strengths of both worlds to realize a completely new yet familiar way of being in communion. In order to realize a new way of being a church attained from the two inherited worlds, Korean immigrants and Korean Americans must take their history seriously, especially their brokenness in Korea leading to their departure; their present realities in a hyphenated reality, especially in their continued brokenness through displacement; and their future hopes, especially in the resettlement as a people building an earthly and heavenly home.

Therefore, *Memory and Honor* will begin with a brief history of the Korean people in their national and religious development. In addition, the immigration history of the Korean people to the U.S. will be examined in both its social and religious context since this plays an intricate part in differentiating and defining Korean Americans Catholics. In particular, *han*, a "debilitating inner spiritual condition" influenced by various aspects of Korean society and culture, will be highlighted as it continues to influence Koreans and Korean Americans alike. Although circumstances, context, or reasons for *han* differ from locale to locale, the debilitating grip on the people of Korean descent is real today regardless of geography. Proper acknowledgment of this condition, in particular, the transformation of *han* as it migrates with the people and passes to the next generation, allows for sensitive social and pastoral responses for Korean Americans.

As the history of Korean Americans further develops over time, models for growth and success, as imperfect and incomplete as they are, begin to emerge. Case studies are presented to illustrate the creative spirit of ministering to Korean Americans as generational issues come to the forefront within a religious context. Models of ministry to immigrants, the 1.5 generation, and the next generation vary depending on geographic locale, concentration of the Korean American population, material resources, and clergy support since missioners from different dioceses of Korea as well as Korean American clergy have competing pastoral visions. By highlighting some hopeful models of Korean American ministry, we are able to see how the church is able to respond to a specific Asian American population defined by its complex yet rich heritage.

Through the complexity of their Korean history, the added pressures through the displacement of the immigration process, and the continuing stresses of resettlement, especially on subsequent generations, Korean Americans have become distinct in their psychological profile while resembling those across the Pacific. Because of their unique history as an immigrant group and a minority, Korean Americans now are distinguished outside their own ethnic enclave by government agencies, while internally being disconnected through the lived experienced on U.S. soil. Therefore, Korean Americans are becoming a unique group now capable of gleaning the richness from their home country of Korea and their host country of the U.S. Both societies and both cultures today offer many resources and opportunities. Therefore, this book concludes with today's pastoral and social challenges to Korean American Catholics.

Just as the U.S. government has moved to identify people of Korean descent living in the U.S. as its own citizens, the church must also respond to this specific group of people rather than treat them as offshoots of the population of Korea or people waiting to be integrated into English-speaking communities. By examining the past, the hope is to provide a framework for the future. With the rise of pastoral challenges as immigrants are caught in between two worlds and as generations mature and clash with one another, opportunities to root themselves as people of Korean descent living in the U.S. and as part of the Catholic Church are coming into fruition. This realization is not just the gift of Korean Americans, or Koreans in general, but humanity's gift as issues of displacement and resettlement affect all human beings.

CHAPTER 1

A Korean American Reality

Sunday, April 29, 2012, was like any other day here in the U.S. Many Americans enjoyed their rest over the weekend, went to the stores for their usual shopping urges, and simply went about their everyday lives. Even those of Korean descent living here went about their day without much attention to the real significance of this day. Many Koreans went to church with their families, shopped at the local Korean market for their weekly dietary needs, and most likely shared a meal with family and friends at a neighborhood restaurant or at home. Thus, Sunday, April 29, was like most Sundays, a day to enjoy friends and family and to take care of personal matters at the end of a busy week. However, this Sunday was not like any other day as Sunday, April 29, 2012, marked the twentieth anniversary of the Los Angeles riots—a local event packed with social implications for the rest of the nation and the entire world, for that matter, with the rise of globalization and immigration—that has not been properly addressed.

News reports highlighting the twentieth anniversary continue to reveal how out of touch we are as a nation to the events known to the Korean American community as *Sa-i-gu* (429 in Korean to mark the April 29 event). Headlines focused on key figures who ignited the L.A. riots; however, these were not necessarily the central themes at the end of the rioting. What failed to appear center stage in remembering the L.A. riots twenty years later was the devastation the people of Korean descent suffered in the midst of unleashed anger and chaos not just on a specific date twenty years ago but still ongoing today. Korean immigrants living and working in targeted areas of Los Angeles suffered unimaginable physical damage as buildings were burned to the ground and indelible emotional scars as the country they once considered their new home seemed to reject them as outsiders. The psychological and emotional scars from treatments by their own neighbors as well as the rest of the country were an incredible setback still requiring local and national healing.

On the surface, the L.A. riots appeared to focus on local issues of race (black residents and Korean American business owners) and injustice (Rodney King and police brutality). However, issues of race and injustice raised in the neighborhood rioting had deeper implications for the entire country and other parts of the world in the face of increasing global migration. On the one hand, this anniversary signified a great tragedy in this country as the African American community along with the media targeted Korean immigrants and their offspring in the Los Angeles area. This event horrified a nation as brothers and sisters professing similar civil and religious beliefs transgressed against one another and as a whole country watched passively as several communities were brutally brought to their knees. On the other hand, this event sparked a consciousness within the Korean community but one that is still waiting to come to fruition today. As Korean Americans living in the U.S. deepen their heritage, the immigrant and subsequent generations are slowly gaining a consciousness of their identity, culture, and linguistic expressions, albeit through tragic events. However, even with such tragedies, Korean Americans have the opportunity to transform events such as *sa-i-gu* into a positive expression and thus, a significant contribution of healing and reconciliation to overall church and society.

Many could argue that the L.A. riots pale in comparison to this country's other race-related events, such as the black or Chicano civil rights movements of the sixties. Others would also argue that as a national tragedy, the L.A. riots pale in comparison to events such as the 9/11 terrorist attacks on the World Trade Center that gripped the entire world watching the Twin Towers fall one at a time. Yes, some could argue that the rioting in Southern California is simply an anomaly or a result of the conditions found locally. However, the significance of this event is quite important since many of the underlying causes of the rioting have not been properly addressed. When there is a local, regional, national, or even international struggle or tragedy, these events are often remembered as a holiday, commemorated in a monument, or celebrated as a religious or civic celebration. The L.A. riots enjoy neither a holiday remembrance, a national structure dedicated to it, nor an annual celebration as a civic or religious occasion. Precisely because it has not gained any attention may prove its invaluable worth to Korean Americans and overall society. This is why the twentieth anniversary of this tragedy is important not only to me as a Korean American but also for this country and for the entire world, for it is an incomplete work awaiting further examination and closure. The truth of this reality and lessons to be learned have yet to be realized within an ethic group and the entire nation. Key issues regarding race and societal injustices have not been properly addressed, resolved, and commemorated from the 1992 riots. Rather, much has been overlooked and kept silent by both mainstream society and the Korean communities—the former misunderstanding such an event as an isolated incidence and the latter ashamed and thus unaware to do so.

Displacement and resettlement are critical issues not only for the immigrants themselves but also for the host countries as diversity increases. "The racial tension between Blacks and Koreans was obviously not the reason for the mass destruction visited upon Los Angeles in 1992. Rather, it was a far more complex set of factors that produced the tragedy of that spring."[4] In particular, the lack of a positive social presence of Korean immigrants in their own communities exposed their rootlessness once they had left their homelands, and without these connections, they became easy scapegoats. As in any vicious cycle, the lack of community roots for Korean immigrants and their children makes them vulnerable to such attacks, while these attacks further exacerbate the rootlessness of the Korean community.

In order for an immigrant or minority group to gain a social consciousness allowing for dialogue and stability in this country requires understanding of its place and contribution to church and society. A certain type of event rallying a particular group together must first occur so that awareness on a greater scale sparks and fuels the conversation. In the case of Korean Americans, as with many ethnic minorities, these rallying moments have been all too painful and tragic, not only with recent events in the country of destination, but also in the events leading up to their departure in their country of origin. Although Korean immigration to the U.S. is more than a century old, it is only the events of the last two decades that have allowed this conversation distinguishing lives here in the U.S. with those abroad.

Few events in the history of Korean Americans have impacted both this ethnic group and the overall population like the Los Angeles riots in 1992. Thus, the L.A. riots left an indelible mark on the U.S. and, in particular, the Korean American community. This tragic event left many immigrants and their poor neighbors to suffer physically and emotionally. In the ashes of burning businesses and neighborhoods rose a generation of Korean Americans giving voice to the then little known

---

[4] Angela E. Oh, "An Issue of Time and Place: The Truth Behind Korean Americans' Connection to the 1992 Los Angeles Riots," *Harvard Journal of Asian American Policy Review* 19 (2010): 44.

Korean American community—other than the stereotypical categories of being a model minority or small-business owner—to the rest of the country. Korean American Protestant ministers rallied their congregations to bring relief to the devastated areas of Los Angeles. In doing so, young Korean American Protestant ministers became a new breed of community leaders because of their English-speaking abilities and organizational skills.[5] Other professionals also came to the forefront for the Korean American community, such as Angela Oh, a lawyer in Los Angeles who recalls becoming a voice not only for those affected by the riots but also for those throughout the country plagued by immigration and ethnic issues. Oh became a community leader of immigrants during the L.A. riots even though she herself was never one, since she was born in the U.S. and had never previously visited Korea. The sheer fact of her Korean appearance was enough for Korean immigrants to place their trust in her.

> During the 1992 riots, Koreans and Korean Americans were viewed interchangeably. This is why it was possible for me, a second-generation Korean American woman born and raised in Los Angeles—who had never even visited the Korean peninsula and who was decidedly progressive and nonreligious at the time—to be identified as "the spokesperson" for the affected community. It happened that the ignorance of the media and the dearth of leadership in Los Angeles opened the way for a relatively young trial lawyer like myself to emerge as a voice. The Koreans of the first generation were stunned, as were the Korean Americans of the second and third generations. The label of "spokesperson" created a drive for more spokespersons to be recognized, and thankfully, today there are many who speak on behalf of the diverse community of ethnic Koreans, both native-born and immigrant.[6]

Oh's reflection almost twenty years later raises another conversation that did not exist in 1992. Today, distinctions are being made between Koreans and Korean Americans. In 1992, Oh was able to represent a whole minority group because of their brief history as immigrants (since the 1965 Immigration Act) and the lack of social consciousness. Two

---

[5] Sharon Kim, *A Faith of Our Own: Second-Generation Spirituality in Korean American Churches* (Piscataway, NJ: Rutgers University Press, 2010), 49.

[6] Oh, "Issue of Time and Place," 46.

decades later, there are visible distinctions being drawn between Koreans and Korean Americans with genetic DNA and Asian appearance no longer the primary factor.

The 2007 Virginia Tech shooting by a Korean American college student is not only another historic moment for Korean Americans but a watershed moment as concrete Korean and Korean American distinctions were made. Although the intensity of the Virginia Tech shooting propelled it into the media, singling out Korean Americans, all cultural groups including Euro-Americans face the challenges of their own members who are unable to adjust to the rigors and pressures of family and society. Regardless of ethnic background, people struggling with personal difficulties exist and act out in various ways. Unfortunately, some of these acts not only harm individuals but also inflict permanent damage on an entire group or nation. It so happened that the Virginia Tech incident exposed the inability of some members of a particular group to cope with life struggles, in particular Korean Americans living within a Korean familial structure encased within the dominant society. Thus, the Virginia Tech tragedy provided an uneasy platform similar to, yet different from, the L.A. riots for Korean American cultural and generational awareness. Culturally, Koreans and their descendants living in the U.S. are identified within different categories, bringing about distinctions not previously drawn. Generationally, the first, the 1.5 (those who came at an early age), and the second generations of Korean Americans were forced to examine their identities and their relationships to one another.

In the past, the Korean government apologized for any suffering caused by people of Korean descent outside their homeland. Regardless of one's global location, those living in the diaspora were considered Korean. "When it was discovered that the gunman was from a Korean family, the Korean government tried to send a delegation to offer condolences, but the U.S. State Department declined. They said their decision was based on the fact that America is a multi-ethnic country, and as such would be uncomfortable having representatives of another government take an ethnic approach to the shooting."[7] In addition, continual U.S. involvement in the Korean peninsula along with this delineation of Korean and Korean Americans continues to divide rather than unite. "It is clear that

---

[7] Kim Gi-bong, "The Legacy of Cho Seung-hui: America's Lesson to Koreans," *Korea JoongAng Daily*, April 25, 2007, accessed August 24, 2011, http://watchingamerica.com/joongangdaily000036.shtml.

the history of U.S. intervention has ruptured the ties between South Korean nationalism and Korean American nationalism."[8]

Although the U.S. government specifically distinguishes Koreans and Korean Americans in this situation, others are also beginning to ask questions disconnecting into two that which for so long were seen as one and the same. Although immigrants and their offspring find it much more consoling and easy to refer to themselves as Korean rather than a hyphenated identity, Korean Americans are becoming an increasingly noticeable people with differing characteristics than those of their homeland. Whether as an immigrant, 1.5, or second generation, what differentiates internally and externally are the cultural influences of the U.S. Often, generational differences among immigrants and their offspring are contributed to the length of exposure to the new environment. Thus, when differences become apparent between Koreans and Korean Americans and among the Korean immigrant generations, it is commonly attributed to their time away from Korea. Thus, as Korean Americans naturally become distanced from the cultural and historical events of Korea because of their lives in the U.S., further characteristics distinguishing the two will increase. The Virginia Tech incident is a watershed moment delineating the Korean and Korean American reality. In addition, some of the distinctions being made between Koreans and Korean Americans are also coming from the country of origin as Korean presence in a global economy is primarily attributed to the advances on the Korean peninsula and not dependent on the Korean diaspora in the U.S., as previously might have been the case. Today, genetic factors are secondary as the U.S. provides a different environment, and as a result, Korean Americans may look like their Asian counterparts but act, speak, and think very differently at times.

Today's Korean Immigrant and Korean American Catholic Reality

The incredible growth of the Catholic Church in Korea in recent years is a hopeful sign for Christianity throughout the world. In particular, the rapid rise of the Catholic population in Korea is a positive experience for Catholicism in Asia and a model of growth everywhere. Whereas the faith in other Asian countries has been silenced, remained stagnant, or is in decline with demographic and cultural shifts, Catholicism in Korea

---

[8] Min-Jung Kim, "Moments of Danger in the (Dis)continuous Relation of Korean Nationalism and Korean American Nationalism," *Positions* 5, no. 2 (1997): 379.

has experienced unprecedented growth with over five million Catholics today. This growth has excelled in the face of technological and social advances, a trend contrary to many Christian experiences in other parts of the world. Thus, not only are the numbers of Catholics impressive and the mega-churches numerous, but also the cultural and societal acceptance of a fairly recent religious experience makes Catholicism in Korea a dynamic and exemplary moment in salvation history.

Although recent advances of Catholicism in Korea are wonderful signs for the entire church, the Catholicism of Korean descent in the U.S. have not had the same luxury as their counterpart. Later chapters will examine some of the factors contributing to this disparity; however, it is important to understand here that the Korean immigrant experience of Catholicism is one of stark contrast. Rather than experiencing a similar meteoric rise in membership and unprecedented social acceptance, the Catholic experience for the Korean immigrant church has been living a stepchild-like existence. The stepchild-like syndrome has been encountered on two levels. First, the Korean Catholic communities initially formed by the immigrant generation have been seen as an anomaly by mainstream churches, leading most of these ethnic communities to establish their own church, structures, and programs. Second, with the rise of the Catholic Church in Korea, especially with vocations to the priesthood, missioners who will return to Korea in four years or less minister to most of the communities formed here, lending to further instabilities. The disparity of Catholicism in leadership, membership, structures, and locations here often leads missioners to view the immigrant communities as inferior. Comparisons to the church back in Korea in terms of congregation size as well as clergy constantly remind Korean immigrants and the next generation Catholics of their shortcomings.

Although the disparity of the church between the immigrant communities and their counterpart back home does not mean that those living in the diaspora did not have a contribution in the developments of the Catholic Church in Korea. Until the recent economic upturn in Korea, many immigrants, especially those in the U.S., not only supported the overall development of Korea but also sustained the church's welfare. Thus, the history of the Catholic Church must acknowledge the invaluable and often unmentioned contributions to the communal developments that make the church universal. For example, many priests and religious sisters appealed to the immigrant communities in the U.S. for financial support of their communities and building projects in Korea. In addition, many priests studying in Europe and the U.S. received financial assistance in their educational endeavors. Even today, as Korea sends missioners to other parts of the world, the immigrant generation here in the U.S. supports their causes. Thus, those separated from the recent Catholic phenomenon in Korea should not continue their inferior status in the diaspora but rather take pride in both their past and ongoing contributions to the rise of Catholicism in Korea and worldwide.

That being said, the Korean immigrant Catholic communities and the next generations of Korean Americans are experiencing an unknown reality compared to their Catholic counterpart in Korea. One of the main issues facing clergy missioners from Korea is that the U.S. Catholic reality, even for Korean immigrants and the next generation, is constantly in a transitional state. The U.S. Catholic Church has been one of immigrants, first from Europe and today from Asia and Latin America. Thus, the influx of immigrants changing the face of the U.S. Catholic Church presents wonderful opportunities and ongoing challenges. Decline in membership, lack of ministerial spaces, shortage of clergy and lay leadership, great distances of travel, and, most importantly, the lack of the next generation in the immigrant churches are just some of the challenges facing most ethnic groups in the U.S. Even in the face of these great challenges, many more opportunities for growth and contributions to the universal church, overall society, and the global community are ever present. But to realize the opportunities and potential of this ethnic group requires much reflection so that a dialogue can first take place. Through such theological and social reflection the church will have something to say to the immigrant generation and those emerging in hyphenated realities, and in turn these groups will continue the life of the church.

In particular, theological and sociological reflections are needed with the Korean Catholic population to document trends of the initial generation who built the church buildings, ongoing immigration due to a global economy, and the religious transmission of faith to subsequent generations. After decades of growth for most faith communities, the Catholic Church of Korean heritage in the U.S. has leveled off according to the latest census data. In 2006, there were 90,250 parishioners in 172 communities scattered throughout the country.[9] Today, the Korean American Priest Association (KAPA) estimates a little over 91,000 parishioners are part of 178 ecclesial communities. This is a disturbing

---

[9] Anselm Kyongsuk Min, "Korean American Catholic Communities," in *Religion and Spirituality in Korean America*, ed. David Yoon and Ruth Chung (Champaign: University of Illinois Press, 2008), 21.

trend given the growth of the Catholic population in Korea as well as the Protestant faithful here in the U.S.

This trend, however, does not mean ethnic churches or communities in the Catholic faith are not needed as before. Rather, this disturbing statistic signifies a couple of developments. First, as the rate of the Korean American population increases, the decrease in the Korean American Catholic population means that the faith is not being passed on to the next generation in significant enough numbers. One of the constant complaints with Korean Catholic immigrants and the next generation is the lack of ministries and ownership of Korean American young adults. In addition, with ongoing U.S. immigration, Korean immigrants are finding their spiritual homes in Protestant rather than Catholic circles, since a majority of Korean Americans still profess a Judeo-Christian belief. Finally, we can surmise that the contradictory trends of Korean population growth in the U.S. and the decline of Korean American Catholics means that the ministerial outreach to this immigrant group is insufficient by the local Korean American communities, the dioceses or archdioceses where these communities reside, and the overall pastoral vision of the U.S. Catholic Church.

Arguments can be made with the declining numbers of Catholics of Korean descent that they are simply following previous trends—similar to European immigrants who no longer needed ethnic parishes when their children either went to English Mass with no cultural distinction or simply did not practice the faith any longer. The difference today is that immigration is still occurring for different reasons than those of the past, but it is still a reality. The need for social and cultural ties in a foreign land is still the primary reason for seeking spiritual reprieve in a disjointed situation as a result of immigration. Unlike the European counterparts whose country of origin also witnessed significant declines in church membership, the Korean religious experience has been the opposite. The rapid and influential rise of Catholicism in overall Korean society must also translate somehow to those living in the diaspora, especially since the Catholic communities in the U.S. are intimately tied to the ecclesial situation in Korea.

The primary lessons to be gleaned from recent statistical trends are that the Korean Catholic experience in the U.S. is first and foremost a different reality resembling the religious experiences of both the homeland and their new home. Second, because of resemblances the people in the diaspora carry on the practices and traditions which are the best and most important aspects of one's cultural faith. However, the differences also remind us that we must reevaluate and re-create a new vision of pastoral ministry that directly speaks to the immigrant situation in the U.S. where Korean Americans are caught in between two worlds, two languages, and even two churches. Finally, we must respect and value the experience of the newly developing ecclesial and social identities of Korean Americans as authentic expressions of both church and as citizens. Korean Americans are definitely in a state of flux from both the perspectives of their country of origin and their country of destination. However, this state should not be seen as something "less than" or something still to come. Rather, out of this state of fluctuation will arise a more mature people who are nonetheless still the same people today.

CHAPTER 2

Remembering the History of Catholicism in Korea

A romantic notion of remembering becomes evident when looking back on the history of Korean Catholicism or Korean history in general. Koreans have a somewhat inferior psyche as a result of having their country conquered and occupied by both China and Japan along with a long history of personal and communal tragedies. This is often referred to as *han* in their historical reflections. However, the successes arising from these underdog conditions are greatly upheld and recounted with much affinity. Outside of these successful moments, in-depth personal accounts are rare because of the pain and shame associated with such devastating experiences. The introduction and survival of Catholicism in Korea is one of the great successes not only for Koreans but also for Christianity as a whole.

From the very beginning, the Christian faith was spread by the preaching of the Gospel: "But how can they call on him in whom they have not believed? And how can they believe in him of whom they have not heard? And how can they hear without someone to preach?" (Rom 10:14, NAB). In the case of Korea, there were no missioners initially proclaiming the Christian message on native soil. The Catholic faith was not planted by clergy or other missioners, as found elsewhere; rather, Christianity took root in Korea through the curiosity and initiative of the natives themselves, through the faith of the laity. Through their contact with Catholics and doctrinal texts from China, the first Korean Christians embraced the faith through their own efforts.

Catholicism in the Late Chosŏn Dynasty

For centuries a 'Hermit Kingdom', in the late nineteenth century Chosŏn was forced to come to terms with the nations which for

23

their own purposes sought to bring her out of her isolation. After considerable dickering, the Japanese forced on the Korean government the first Western-style treaty, the Treaty of Kanghwa in 1876. This treaty was followed by treaties with the United States in 1882, with the United Kingdom and the German Empire in 1883, and with other European nations shortly afterwards. . . . One important point to observe about the period from 1870 to 1900 is that all foreign powers treated Korea as a pawn to be moved about at will, which is some indication of the politically and physically weak state of the dynasty. The 500-year-old Chosŏn Dynasty was near collapse, as also was the traditional structure of society.[1]

Catholicism was first introduced to Koreans as early as the sixteenth century and then by missioners in the late nineteenth century.[2] The encounter with Catholicism is traditionally categorized into three historical periods.[3] The first period where Korean scholars encountered the works of Westerners such as those of Jesuit missioners was known as the acceptance of Catholicism, beginning in early sixteenth century and lasting until 1784. The period of persecution from 1785 to 1886 witnessed numerous martyrs as the Catholic Church began laying the foundation for future generations. After the devastating persecutions of 1886, the Catholic Church enjoyed relative religious freedom during the era of religious liberty.

During the reign of King Sŏn-jo from 1568 to 1608, emissaries visiting the court of the Chinese emperor in Peking brought many books on the Catholic faith back to Korea. Some accounts recall this interest in Catholicism as a quest for the true religion.[4] Others summarize the

---

[1] James Huntley Grayson, *Korea: A Religious History* (London: RoutledgeCurzon, 2002), 149–50.

[2] "Although there are records that the Jesuit priest Gregorio de Cespedes was sent to Korea during the Japanese Hideyoshi invasion (1592–98) to minister to the Japanese soldiers (where he is claimed to have baptized more than two hundred abandoned children), his putative presence had no effect on the subsequent practice of Catholicism in Korea" (Inshil Choe Yoon, "Martyrdom and Social Activism: The Korean Practice of Catholicism," in *Religions of Korea in Practice*, ed. Robert Buswell [Princeton, NJ: Princeton University Press, 2007], 355).

[3] Jai-Keun Choi, *The Origin of the Roman Catholic Church in Korea: An Examination of Popular and Governmental Responses to Catholic Missions in the Late Choson Dynasty* (Seoul, Korea: Hermit Kingdom Press, 2006), 4.

[4] Joseph Chang-mun Kim and John Jae-sun Chung, eds., *Catholic Korea: Yesterday and Today* (Seoul, Korea: Catholic Korea, 1964), 18.

initial encounter of Catholicism more out of a curiosity for Western culture since Catholicism was initially referred to as *Sŏhak* or Western Learning. The West was seen as an alternative to Chinese government and society as people in the Korean peninsula sought independence from their neighbors to the east.

> After the invasion of Japan and China, Korean intellectuals sought new thought, religion, and other cultural enrichments. These desires were satisfied through newly introduced Western books. Many Korean intellectuals came to respect the Western world and adopted a new world view contrary to the traditional China-centered world view. Over a century they read and studied Western books and a certain group of Korean intellectuals came to accept a Western religion (so-called the Western Learning) and confessed the Christian faith. They founded a Christian church by themselves without the aid of missionaries.[5]

In 1631, Chŏng Tu-wŏn was one of the first to encounter the Catholic faith from foreigners in China and bring the experience back to his homeland. Through his interactions, Chŏng Tu-wŏn was able to acquire many Western gifts along with his newfound knowledge of Catholicism. "Approximately 167 envoys of various purposes were dispatched during the 147 years, up to 1783. . . . Items brought back by the Korean envoys ranged greatly in their variety: Catholic doctrinal books translated into Chinese, books on astronomy, geography and mathematics, world maps, sundials, telescopes, and musical instruments."[6] Regardless of whether the initial interest in Catholicism stemmed from interests in Western culture or in the search for a true religion, scholars can all agree that the embrace of Catholicism by the learned class allowed the first roots to be deepened on native soil.

The first written Korean account detailing an encounter with Catholicism was in *The Essays of Chi-pong* by Lee Su-kwang. In his reflections, Lee Su-kwang mentions his reading of Matteo Ricci's *Tianzhu shiyi*, or *The True Meaning of the Doctrine of Heaven and Earth*. Although the Chinese people did not refer to God in the same manner as Westerners did, Ricci was still able to connect the Chinese belief of heaven and earth with the Judeo-Christian notion of the divine. Ricci's influential work allowed

[5] Choi, *The Origin*, 324.
[6] Ibid., 19.

many in China to embrace Catholicism once it was seen as compatible with their Confucian form of government and society. Upon bringing Ricci's *Tianzhu shiyi* back to Korea, many of the Korean *Shilhak* scholars studied the text in the hopes of further understanding the Western world. The interest in Western culture eventually led to Korea's contact and the spread of Christianity.

Out of further curiosity, *Shilhak* scholars requested that more information about the Catholic faith be ascertained from China. In 1784, the son of the Korean ambassador to China, Peter Seung-hun Yi (Yi Sŭnghun), encountered a Chinese Catholic priest in Beijing and his inquiries eventually led to his own baptism. With newfound faith, Yi returned to Korea to pass on the faith by transporting texts across the closely guarded border and sharing his personal experiences. Soon after, many who became believers crossed over to China several times to grow in their faith under dangerous conditions. Much of Ricci's foundational work bridging Catholicism and Confucianism came to an abrupt end during the Rites Controversy in the eighteenth century, when the papacy no longer tolerated the Chinese reference to God in their own cultural terminology and cosmology. Since then, Christianity was suspiciously regarded in Asia because of the apparent conflict of ancestor worship with Catholic monotheistic beliefs; however, this was not the case with the newly converted believers, as they were able to reconcile the two.

The encounter with the West through doctrinal Catholic writings did not prove to be controversial for the early Christians on the Korean peninsula. The lack of conflict between Korean Confucian beliefs and Catholic doctrine was attributed to the missing catechetical element usually found when missioners are the first to spread the gospel message. Thus, without outside influences, the early believers on Korean soil naturally felt at home with their newfound Catholic beliefs and their Confucian cultural identity as they created a system where the two were able to coexist. To the first converts on the peninsula, these two systems were never initially viewed in conflict or contradicting one another. Being on their own religiously, isolated on a peninsula physically, without any foreign missioners or initial contact in encountering the faith also meant that their own rationale was sufficient. Their own lived experiences with Catholicism and Confucianism, no matter how brief, were enough as both tenets helped the Korean people love their newly discovered God as well as be in right relationships with one another. It was not until 1790 that this early Christian community realized the questions of compatibility between the Catholic faith and their Confucian thought, especially when it came to honoring deceased family members. Not until a French bishop wrote directly on this matter did Koreans with their newfound faith question whether or not a conflict existed between the use of ancestral tables in Confucian memorial services and their Catholic practices.

> The emergence of Catholicism on the peninsula marked the first time Koreans accepted a personal and loving God as the creator of the universe, who incarnated and suffered for humanity's salvation. Their reverence of God above as the Great King and father (*taegun taebu*) and the Great Parent (*taebumo*), superior even to the king and family, clashed with the principles of loyalty and filial piety that are so central to Neo-Confucianism. In addition, it challenged the political authority of the Court.[7]

In obedience to the French bishop, many Catholics resisted societal pressures to continue the rituals required by Confucianism and instead chose to either burn or bury their ancestral tablets next to the graves of their deceased family members. These acts of defiance of ancestral worship forced governmental officials to retaliate in order to safeguard their long-standing societal traditions. By withholding ceremonial rituals that included the use of wooden tablets containing the names of deceased family members and also from offering food and wine to the deceased spirit, Catholics were viewed as being unfaithful to, and even completely abandoning, their filial duties. Thus, the first persecutions of Catholics in Korea became a campaign to preserve Confucian customs through the eradication of the newly introduced Catholic beliefs that appeared to challenge Confucian-based society. The first persecutions resulted in either apostasy for the first believers or bloody martyrdom on Korean soil as the choice between one's belief in family and one's belief in God became irreconcilable in society.

Nowhere else did Christianity spread in this manner, as missioners were invited into Korea only after the neophytes understood for themselves the need for ordained clergy in the celebration of the sacraments. After a decade of living out the faith in isolation from the universal church, the faithful in Korea became aware of the constitutive relationship between the ordained clergy and sacraments; however, they continued their religious practices, in particular, the consecration of the Eucharist by lay leaders, until missioners finally arrived. For new believers it was

[7] Yoon, "Martyrdom," 357.

more important to live out a sacramental life even without a priest than to wait for a priest without regular reception of the sacraments. The fear of living without the real presence of Jesus in their spiritual lives and even dying without this sacramental reality was too great to overcome. The first converts felt it necessary to live out their faith sacramentally in their own way, even if it was an aberration, than to go without.

It was not until 1794 when a Chinese priest, Father James Chou, crossed over to Korea from China to minister to the newly formed Catholic community that the Korean Church would finally have clergy presence. In 1795, the Korean Catholic community of Chosŏn celebrated their first Mass with Fr. Chou presiding. This religious event in Korean Catholic history was likened to Jesus' own baptism. As the Spirit descended on Jesus at the river Jordan, a priest in their midst resembled another gift flowing down from the heavens for the nascent church. Catholicism in the Chosŏn region began formally taking shape with a clergy presence and Koreans' unique acceptance of Christianity. The local community was now fully part of the universal church with her prayers and beliefs. Fr. Chou served this community until his martyrdom in 1801. In 1795, the Korean Catholic Church consisted of four thousand members. Within six years, the faithful grew to ten thousand believers in 1801.

Although the Catholic faith was suspiciously looked upon after the Rites Controversy, King Chongjo of Korea still tolerated the believers of this new faith. However, his death in 1799 also signaled the end of toleration for the Catholic faith as more persecutions broke out. By 1801, three hundred faithful died for their faith with another thousand arrested for their beliefs. During this period of Catholic persecution, another Chinese priest, Father Liu Fangchi, arrived in Korea in 1831 to continue the priestly ministry of the rapidly growing Korean Catholic community. The establishment of Korea as a prefecture apostolic in 1831 by Pope Leo XII allowed Monsignor Lawrence Imbert and other missioners from the Paris Foreign Missions Society to arrive in Korea in 1836. By 1839, a full-scale persecution of the Catholic faith led to several martyrdoms of both European missioners and native believers.

Andrew Taegon Kim and Thomas Yang Eop Choe

Andrew Taegon Kim was the first native Korean priest ordained in 1845, and his priestly ministry lasted only a short duration, with his martyrdom in 1846. Today, he is revered above all the Korean martyrs. It is interesting to point out that there are few parishes named after

Andrew Taegon Kim (Kim Taegŏn) in Korea with many of the churches devoted to other non-Korean saints throughout history. In addition, many parishes are simply referred to by their neighborhood districts in Korea. However, almost every state in the U.S. has at least one Korean American Catholic parish, center, or community named after this saint. Andrew Kim symbolizes the immigrants' way of identifying themselves as both Catholics and Koreans. There are several reasons why this saint stands out from the other canonized martyrs in Korean history. As the first native clergy in a very hierarchical society even today, his death by beheading captures the imagination of the fallen hero sacrificing himself for others in a manner similar to that of Jesus. The martyrdom of Andrew Taegon Kim symbolizes the honor and success of Korean Catholicism. Under heavy persecution, Andrew Taegon Kim is an underdog figure who rises to success, not because of his known accomplishments, but because he embodies the Korean ideals of overcoming suffering, persecution, tragedies—in short, overcoming *han*. What also contributes to his following is the widespread and rapid growth of Catholicism in Korea today. Modern successes in the church, such as the growing numbers of vocations and laity, are now attributed to the selfless acts of the one who paved the way. Although many lost their lives on behalf of the faith during several periods of persecution, Andrew Taegon Kim still stands out, symbolizing the way Koreans want to remember their past and overcome their tragedies.

In contrast, Thomas Yang Eop Choe (Ch'oe Yangŏp), the second native priest of Korea, did not die a martyr's death but a "natural" one at the hands of typhoid in 1861. Soon after his ordination in 1849, Thomas Yang Eop Choe became known as the "martyr of sweat" because of the over seventeen hundred miles he traveled and four thousand confessions he administered yearly. Yet today, he is rarely recognized in comparison to Andrew Taegon Kim, the "martyr of blood," and his canonization is still in waiting, along with another 124 Korean martyrs in Rome. Thomas will be the first Korean Catholic non-martyred saint once canonized. Without wildly speculating on the rational for the differences of recognition between Andrew and Thomas, one can use these two figures to illustrate the way Koreans remember or fail to remember the past.

There is little doubt that Thomas has done more in the promulgation of the church in Korea than Andrew.

> He spent most of his time visiting the 127 Catholic settlements scattered in five provinces. He wrote Catholic verses (*Ch'ŏnju kasa*),

including "Sahyangga" (Hymn of Longing for Home), using the traditional *kasa* form, in which each unit of verse is arranged into four groups of mainly four syllables. Reciting verses proved to be an easy method of indoctrination, and the recitation of *Ch'ŏnju kasa* was handed down to younger generations and served as a tool of educating children at home.[8]

Because of the longevity of his ministry, his presence made much more of an impact on the infant church. However, his ordinary, "un-heroic," and unfortunate ending does not capture the imagination of Koreans in their reflections. Andrew Taegon Kim, by being the first native priest and dying a martyr's death, embodies many of the ideals Koreans of Catholic descent strive for. Similar to other attributes praised in Korean society, Catholics seek an ideal situation or person where there are no equals and, therefore, no way of comparisons. Thus, there will be no rivaling Andrew Taegon Kim's position of being the first native priest, the first native clergy martyred, and among the first to be canonized a saint. Arguably, there is no other single Catholic figure in Korea who can rival Andrew's status. Thus, Andrew Taegon Kim is revered by the masses and has had many churches dedicated to him while Thomas Yang Eop Choe is still awaiting recognition for his contributions.

All told, numerous persecutions took place throughout this early period of Korean Catholicism. "The first persecution occurred in 1785. It was followed by the Sinhae Persecution in 1791, the Ŭlmyo Incident in 1801, the Ŭlhae Persecution in 1815, the Chŏnghae Persecution in 1827, the Kihae Persecution in 1839, the Pyŏngo Persecution in 1846, the Kyŏngsin Persecution in 1860, and lastly by the Pyŏngin Persecution in 1866."[9] The 1866 persecution was so devastating that it reduced the Korean Catholic population in half. Over eight thousand Korean Catholics gave their lives for the faith, including French missioners. In a little less than a decade, in 1873, King Kojong came to power and with his rule came relative peace for Catholics in Korea. By 1910, the Korean Catholic Church consisted of sixty-nine churches with seventy-one foreign missioners, fifteen native priests, fifty-nine religious sisters, and forty-one seminarians to serve the seventy-three thousand faithful.

The unique beginnings of Korean Catholicism may be the key to why Christianity endured in this part of East Asia while religious activities

[8] Ibid., 361.
[9] Choi, *The Origin*, 1n1.

dissipated in China and Japan. If anything, the missionary activities in those countries would have solidified Catholicism during the persecutions. Rather, the opposite occurred as the initiative of the laity propelled the faith to endure through turbulent times.

> One of the special aspects of Korea's acceptance of Catholicism was that the various religious activities centered on lay people, by whom Catholicism was accepted, by whom persecution was endured, and through whom the church grew and developed. Consequently, they were able to endure the persecutions through the power of their own internal strength. Although Korea was a Confucian culture along with China and Japan, persecution did not drive the Korean Catholic Church to degenerate as the church in China did, or disappear as the church in Japan did; on the contrary, the faith of the Korean Catholic believers deepened with the persecution, and the number of followers increased.[10]

Catholicism under Japanese Colonial Rule

With Catholicism being tolerated in the early 1900s in Korea, church activity or membership did not increase at the same rate or fervor prior in this relative calm. Foreign bishops and clergy took a more cautious approach in society, fearing a return to when Catholicism was outlawed. Thus, church leadership began assembling those who were scattered and hiding in mountainous regions by establishing parishes where the Catholic Church could become a central haven. With previous persecutions of the late Chosŏn Dynasty still fresh in the people's consciousness, the Catholic Church played an important role in the private lives and internal healing of loss of property, family, and loved ones in their community. "This type of spirituality engendered in these circumstances was one that emphasized distance from, not participation in, the world. In other words, Catholicism became a religion that merely looked forward to rewards to be experienced in the next life."[11]

Some scholars note the importance of Catholic influence in society especially during the Japanese occupation of Korea.[12] However, the mention of Catholic influence during the first half of the twentieth century is

---

[10] Ibid., 327.
[11] Ibid., 335.
[12] Yoon, "Martyrdom," 362.

largely based on individual Catholic activity and not as a congregational effort led by the Catholic hierarchy. "The Catholic Church did not officially take an active role in the resistance against Japanese colonialism. However, individual Catholics expressed their defiance by joining the March First Independence Movement of 1919, the independent Korean armies that formed in Manchuria, and the provisional government of Korea in Shanghai."[13]

The inactivity of church hierarchy as a communal organization spearheading the charge in the anticolonial protest against Japan can be attributed to a variety of reasons. Regardless, the inactivity of the church in the early 1900s will forever label Catholics as being calloused in their response and would take half a century to overcome even though many individuals actively opposed Japanese rule. The passive position of the Catholic Church at the start of this century has led some scholars to describe Catholic thinking in this period as a "ghetto mentality."[14] By embracing a "ghetto mentality," Catholics separated themselves from mainstream society and concern for the future of society as a whole since most of the church's energies went into maintaining a church that had just undergone the martyrdom of thousands of their brothers and sisters.

Since church leadership did not impact the public sector of government and society, especially when it came to Korea's independence movement against Japan in 1919, the Protestants emerged at the forefront in the people's struggle for freedom and independence throughout the first half of the twentieth century. Perhaps their public involvement during critical moments in Korean nationalism allowed the Protestant churches, and not the Catholic Church, to become the main Christian denomination today. In addition to the Protestant support of nationalism, Protestant missionaries came from the U.S., bringing their Puritan and capitalistic work ethics. Missioners were instrumental in the spread of the Protestant faith, just as the scholars were in promoting Catholicism. For example, John Ross was the first to successfully translate Scripture into Korean, which became invaluable in the spread of the Protestant faith and still influences Korean religious thought today. "The significance of the Ross Translation is twofold: (1) it was the only complete Korean translation of the New Testament until 1900, when the translation of the New Testament done by the Korean missionaries was completed;

---

[13] Ibid.
[14] Grayson, *Korea*, 171–76.

(2) it introduced key theological terms which are still in use today. With regard to the latter point, it is significant that it was Ross who selected the term for God, *Hananim*, a pure Korean word for the Ruler of Heaven."[15]

Protestantism gained a firm foothold in the early part of the century also with its social consciousness. Not only was Korean patriotism supported against Japanese occupation, but also schools and hospitals became important vehicles in promoting Christianity. There were also several key political figures who embraced their Protestant faith in the public forum.

> In their leadership capacities, they advocated Christian civilization and the role it could play in creating a new, modern Korea. Yun Ch'iho wrote in his diary (February 19, 1983) that "Christianity is the salvation and hope of Corea [Korea]." Yi Sŭngman, who became the first president of the Republic of Korea in 1948, explicitly claimed in *Sinhak wŏlbo* (1903) that "Christianity is the foundation of the future of Korea." Assuming that Christian ethics would be the basis for advanced civilization and enlightenment, these converted Korean intellectuals advocated new gender relations that were not only faithful to Christian ways but also in keeping with the nationalist project toward modernity.[16]

Thus, the public Protestant campaign against the Japanese occupation of Korea is just one of several factors that led to a "perfect storm" where the initial Catholic presence did not succeed in becoming the primary Korean Christian denomination.

A serious factor of consideration in regression of Catholic influence in society during the beginnings of the twentieth century was the shift in leadership in the laity. The *yangban* class, the educated elite of society, spearheaded the initial interest and spread of Catholicism in Korea during the late Chosŏn Dynasty. With their intellectual abilities within a communal enterprise, the *yangban* leadership endured years of persecution through their adherence to a religion they discerned to be the correct path in life. In addition, the *yangban* class was also able to organize the first liturgies and catechesis because of their social status and intellectual abilities. Even though many were attracted to the Catholic faith in

---

[15] Ibid., 156.

[16] Hyaeweol Choi, "A New Moral Order: Gender Equality in Korean Christianity," in *Religions of Korea in Practice*, ed. Robert Buswell (Princeton, NJ: Princeton University Press, 2007), 411.

Chosŏn society because of its egalitarian social and ecclesial character since mainstream society during those days consisted of a rigid hierarchy and social structure, the *yangban* class was still instrumental in maintaining the initial Catholic character for all social classes. However, this leadership from the well-educated elite upper class would not continue in the turn of the century.

The Catholic Church during the first half of the 1900s, especially during the Japanese occupation of Korea, did little to promote the involvement of intellectuals in society. The inward focus divorced the Catholic Church from society, one of the main reasons why the *yangban* class first embraced Catholicism since it gave Korea a new way of social, political, and religious expressions. The retreat into the spiritual realm for the Catholic Church did little to promote new intellectuals into their leadership. In fact, the opposite occurred where commoners became the largest portion of the Catholic population. "Furthermore, they point out that the bulk of the converts continued to be drawn from the dispossessed sectors of society with the Church having little attraction to the intelligentsia."[17]

The change in the laity population along with the French missioners' desire for a relatively peaceful existence led to the Catholic Church being undisturbed for most of the colonial period until the very end, at the middle of the twentieth century.

> [T]he Church leadership in Korea would have remembered the sufferings of the first century of the Church and would have feared the onset of another persecution. Consequently, during the late 1930s and early 1940s, when many Protestants were incarcerated and killed over their refusal to participate in State Shintō rituals, there was no Catholic reaction against these rites until 1944 when the acquiescence in a "pagan" rite seems strange in light of the strong stand which the church had taken against participation in the *chesa* ancestral rites.[18]

In addition, the lack of Catholic involvement during Japanese occupation of Korea was also a result of the May 25, 1936, concordat between Rome and Japan. Speaking on behalf of all Catholics, the Vatican issued a statement that reconciled the Japanese State Shintō rites as a patriotic ceremony rather than a religious ritual, thus allowing for Korean Catholic participation. The concordat allowed Korean Catholics under Japanese

---

[17] Grayson, *Korea*, 172.
[18] Ibid., 173.

rule a way to appease those occupying their country while at the same time maintaining their faith. Even with the concordat allowing for Koreans to participate in Japanese State Shintōism and enjoy relative stability and peace, some Catholic leaders and laity still refused to participate in such ceremonies, citing its contradiction with their religious and cultural beliefs. The cost of these protests led to the loss of leadership positions for some clergy members and in other instances the complete closure of the local church.

The combination of all these factors led to the Catholic Church retreating into the background of social concerns while the Protestant churches grew in numbers and influence in the daily lives of the people facing persecution. In particular, Protestants were not only leaders in the campaign against the colonial rule but also leaders in social outreach programs by constructing schools and hospitals, giving Protestants further presence and foothold in Korean society. Thus, the shift in the laity population from the educated elite to mostly commoners left an intellectual void in the Catholic Church. The social and political noninvolvement of French missioners reflecting on the recent persecutions of the early church also did not provide leadership for the Catholic Church as a whole to provide a united front against the Japanese occupation. In addition, the Vatican's involvement in Japanese affairs further complicated Catholic opposition. Given these important developments in Korean Catholicism, the church did not grow and develop as in years prior or after in the post-liberation modern times. Just as the Catholic Church grew under the persecution of the late Chosŏn Dynasty, the Protestant faith grew in light of the new persecutions under Japanese colonial rule.

Catholicism in the Post-Liberation Period

It was not until after the Korean War, in the 1950s, that the Korean Catholic community began to have a significant urban presence. The move from villages to cities, along with enough of an increase in local clergy that Korean priests and bishops finally outnumbered Western missionaries both in parish churches and in bishops' chanceries, brought about dramatic change to Catholicism in Korea. A church that had once been persecuted for refusing to use ancestral tablets in ancestor memorial services now devised its own ritual for honoring ancestors, a ritual that can include a plaque on which the name of the ancestor being honored is written. And a church that once fled from the political arena in fear of its life now speaks out boldly on political issues, if it believes those issues have moral implications. In fact, the Catholic clergy provided many of the leaders of Korea's long but eventually successful fight for democracy, from the 1960s through the 1990s. Myŏngdong Cathedral was once a favorite gathering place for pro-democracy activists.[19]

The religious history of Korea splinters at this point as the Soviet zone of influence in 1945 along with the Communist regime of North Korea annihilated much of the church's activity in the northern half of the Korean peninsula. In addition, detailed accounts of church life are unreliable and negligible at best since the north was and still is today both hostile to organized religion and closed to the outside world. "Control or suppression of the Christian community in the north was important not only because Christians represented a different voice on social and political matters, but because of the size of the Christian community. At this time, the centre of Christianity in Korea was in the north, not the south, an irony of history considering the current size of the Christian Church in South Korea."[20]

While Christianity initially flourished under previous conditions of persecutions, the extreme tyranny in the north was too much for any Christian denomination to endure.

> [The] harsh treatment was not confined to Catholic religious alone but was also characteristic of the way in which the communist regime dealt with the Protestants as well. In 1953, at the time of the cessation of hostilities, the total number of Catholics in South Korea, including many refugees from the north, totaled 166,000 which is ninety percent of the number of Catholics in all of Korea in 1945, which was 183,000. How many secret believers still remained in the north at the time of the truce is not known. However, the statistics do give a dramatic indication of the magnitude of the loss of life during the conflict.[21]

In contrast, Christianity in the south flourished as Catholics increased their civic presence, fulfilling much of the same roles the Protestants

[19] Franklin Rausch and Don Baker, "Catholic Rites and Liturgy," in *Religions of Korea in Practice*, ed. Robert Buswell (Princeton, NJ: Princeton University Press, 2007), 377–78.

[20] Grayson, *Korea*, 162.

[21] Ibid., 174.

had done earlier. Social needs such as educational opportunities, access to medical care, and emergency assistance to those in need became a priority to Catholics during this period.

> More importantly, Catholics became more visibly involved in social outreach than at any time in the past. Unlike the situation in the 1930s, Catholic clergy and laity during the 1970s and 1980s also have been in the forefront of the criticism of the undemocratic, military-style governments. . . . More so than Protestants, Catholics have been noticeably involved in social movements concerned with the welfare of the industrial worker in Korea's rapidly changing society which is undoubtedly a reflection of the roots of the church in the poorer sector of society.[22]

As with everything Catholic, the activities of the local church are somehow supported by the universal church and vice versa. Thus, the growth of the Korean Catholic Church due to the church's social outreach was also fueled by the Second Vatican Council, which allowed such consciousness to develop in the local churches.

> With the opening of the Second Vatican Council (1962–1965) and the Korean church becoming an autonomous hierarchy in 1962, Korean Catholics sought to adjust to contemporary needs. Among the reforms were these radical changes: the Koreanization of rituals, including saying mass in Korean; the active participation of laity in proselytizing; communication with Protestant churches and other religions; and engagement in social and political causes.[23]

In addition, the increase of Korean clergy shifted the "sheltered" mindset of French missioners to a local clergy population engaged with the social and political conditions of the faithful. This increased presence of an indigenous clergy population also meant an urbanization of Catholicism, a presence in contemporary society much different from the church's presence at the turn of the century.

With the rise of the Catholic population in all sectors of society, the Catholic Church was in a position where they could not only voice their opinions in social matters but, more importantly, lead campaigns for social, economic, and political reforms. Previously, the inward focus of the

---

[22] Ibid., 175.
[23] Yoon, "Martyrdom," 363.

Catholic hierarchy at the turn of the century left Catholics without an influence in worldly matters. However, in the second half of the century, the Catholic Church gained a prominent place in the hearts and minds of many Koreans. This shift in the ecclesial presence in society came under the direct leadership of the indigenous clergy population as they began to take up the cause of the exploited working class. Advocating on behalf of farmers, factory laborers, and other exploited workers as Korea embraced Western capitalistic tendencies, the Catholic Church became invaluable in speaking on behalf of those who became lost in the urbanization and industrialization process.

> With the church's present oversized parishes, Catholics are striving for an ongoing renewal, aiming at restoring human dignity and social justice by living as "salt" in a society plagued by rampant materialism. Challenges that Catholics face include the increasing numbers of inactive Catholics, the need for diverse programs for Catholic spirituality, the laity's dependence on the clergy, and the gender imbalance in leadership positions. As members of one of the fastest-growing churches in Asia, Catholics in Korea endeavor to serve a major role in evangelizing Asia and other continents. They are also committed to building closer relationships with Catholics in North Korea and encouraging peace and unification on the Korean peninsula.[24]

The combination of the Second Vatican Council, increase in the indigenous clergy population, and the urbanization of the laity have given Korean Catholics the time and resources to properly reflect on the cultural ramifications of Catholicism on the Korean peninsula. Through local customs of dress, music, and rituals, Catholics have deepened their faith by incorporating the local Korean culture with the universal Catholic faith. "Such adaptation of the nonessentials of Catholic ritual to local traditions is encouraged in the belief that local believers will feel more comfortable with music and clothing that are familiar to them."[25] The conscious blending of Korean traditions with the Catholic tradition is an ongoing dynamic as the universal faith encounters specific people. "This is a deliberate decision to differentiate local practices from those of fellow believers from a different cultural background."[26] The beauty

---

[24] Ibid., 366.
[25] Rausch and Baker, "Catholic Rites," 376.
[26] Ibid., 377.

of Catholicism over the years is the transmission of universal content received within a local context. As the faith continues to spread and deepen within differing cultures, the Catholic faith enriches the local cultures while at the same time being enriched by local understandings.

Also at work within this mutually benefitting dynamic between the local context of Korea and the universal content of Catholicism is an unconscious dynamic. Just as Koreans have consciously chosen dress, music, and rituals of Korean culture to enhance their Catholic experience, unconsciously, Korean Confucian thought, customs, and ideology have also influenced the way Catholics behave in church and society. In many ways, just as Catholicism has christianized Korea, Koreans have "Koreanized" Catholicism. Such Koreanization of Catholicism includes aspects of the Korean faith that are derived from communal experience of the people long before Christianity came to the peninsula. For example, by fusing the Confucian notion of filial piety with the Judeo-Christian understanding found in the Ten Commandments, Koreans are able to maintain their cultural heritage within the framework of Catholicism.

> Catholics all over the world love and honor their parents, of course. Not only is that a normal human emotion, it is also the Fourth Commandment Catholics must obey. However, Koreans go farther than Catholics elsewhere in expressing that love and respect through a specific religious ritual. That is just one aspect of the inculturation that keeps Korean Catholics Korean. Although the Korean Catholic Church is a proud member of a global religious community, it is also proud of its Korean heritage and continues to be both Korean and Catholic.[27]

Summary of Catholicism throughout Korean History

The inward focus of the Catholic Church still recovering from her days of persecution was reflected in the growth of the faithful. In 1910, seventy-three thousand Catholics were reported growing to one hundred thousand by 1930. Twenty years later, the Church saw another 50 percent increase of the laity to 150,000 members in 1950. Although the numbers of faithful grew steadily, this increase pales in comparison to the church's activities of her early days of martyrdom and today's rapid growth. In opposing fashion to the litany of martyrs and struggles of the nineteenth

[27] Ibid., 378.

century of Korean Catholicism, Catholics recalled very little of the activities of the early twentieth century of Korean Catholic Church history.

In 1974, the Korean Catholic Church reached a milestone with a million members. Since then, there has been a rapid rise of Catholics, paralleling both political freedom and economic success of Korean society. The Catholic Church doubled in size to two million by 1985 and took less time to grow to three million by 1992. In 2006, the Korean Catholic Church consisted of three archdioceses and twelve dioceses with a total of 1,476 parishes within them. Overseeing the local church were thirty-two bishops, all native Koreans, along with 3,874 priests serving in various ministries. Although diocesan clergy make up the majority of the presbyterate, there were still 1,444 male religious throughout the country. In addition, there were also 9,770 women religious fulfilling various capacities. The future of the church in Korea also looks bright as 1,380 seminarians filled seven seminaries. Furthermore, over two thousand catechists are educating the next generation of Korean Catholics at local parishes. There were over 4.7 million Catholics representing fewer than 10 percent of the entire Korean population. Today, there are reports of over five million Catholics living in Korea.

From these humble yet unique beginnings, the Catholic Church in Korea has grown quite remarkably and rapidly. Some members of the early Korean Catholic Church were officially recognized for their service and sacrifice by Pope John Paul II in the 1984 canonization of the Korean martyrs, setting September 20 as the feast day of Saints Andrew Kim Taegon, priest, Paul Chong Hasang, and their companions. Although 103 martyrs were officially raised to the level of saints within the Catholic Church, several thousand Christians are estimated to have given their lives for the Catholic faith in Korea. Furthermore, this remarkable occasion is the first time such a canonization has taken place outside of Rome.

> The Korean Church is unique because it was founded entirely by laypeople. This fledgling Church, so young and yet so strong in faith, withstood wave after wave of fierce persecution. Thus, in less than a century, it could boast of 10,000 martyrs. The death of these many martyrs became the leaven of the Church and led to today's splendid flowering of the Church in Korea. Even today their undying spirit sustains the Christians of the Church of Silence in the north of this tragically divided land.[28]

---

[28] Pope John Paul II at the canonization of the Korean martyrs, May 6, 1984.

    In reviewing the ecclesial history of Korea and its unique origins, another interesting aspect of Korean religious culture arises. Beginning with the persecuted Catholics at the introduction of the faith and down to the faithful of today, Koreans identify themselves not only as inheritors of a unique lineage of the local but universal church, but also a history distinguishing Korean Catholics from other religions and even themselves. *Gu gyo* (구 교) is a Korean term derived from Chinese characters; *gu* 舊, representing "old" and *gyo* 敎, "church." With this word construction, Korean Catholics are able to distinguish themselves in two ways. First, Koreans can refer to themselves as *gu gyo* if the Catholic faith has been passed down from generation to generation in their household. This distinction differentiates the longtime Catholic families from neophytes. *Gu gyo* can also be used to distinguish the Catholic Church as the original or longtime presence of Christianity in Korea. "[O]ne could still hear the phrase 'Old Catholics' and 'New Catholics', referring respectively to those people who could trace their ancestry to families which had lived through the period of persecutions, and those who were recent believers and could not trace their spiritual ancestry back to the period of the martyrs."[29] In both cases, *gu gyo* serves to identify, define, and distinguish Koreans within their Catholic faith.

    Gu gyo, by its very nature of identifying those with an extensive household Catholic lineage and those recently admitted into the church, has both a positive and a negative connotation associated with it. Positively, *gu gyo* serves to unify and recognize the first Korean believers who underwent heavy persecution. *Gu gyo* honors the person of faith and their lineage, especially in the struggles of the early Korean Catholic Church. Modern uses of *gu gyo* refer to believers whose faith has been passed down generationally, similar to those labeled as cradle Catholics. My own baptism is an illustration of *gu gyo* as my grandfather took me to daily Mass when I was only five days old and had me baptized without my parents even being there. Many times, my parents would say that my vocation was built upon the foundation of my grandfather's faith. *Gu gyo* connects the Catholic lineage, honoring those who preceded us, similar to the way we trace our biological family tree today.

    Negatively, *gu gyo* separates and reveals Korean bias even within Catholic circles. In order to distinguish, a separation must be made. *Gu gyo* in its institutional use identifies the Korean Catholic Church for its

[29] Grayson, *Korea*, 171.

longevity from other Christian denominations. Individually, *gu gyo* makes a distinction between cradle Catholics and neophytes. Newly baptized Catholics are "reminded" of their recent Catholic lineage, and differences in their mentality further this distinction. For example, Korean cultural holidays may be celebrated differently. *Gu gyo* households tend to observe cultural occasions in a religious manner by going to church. However, a neophyte without such religious household traditions may simply observe cultural events in a secular way. Whether one only visits family members to commemorate an occasion or whether one goes to church before gathering with loved ones may depend on *gu gyo*. Differences such as these in Korean society tend to downplay recently baptized Catholics since they are somehow seen as "unlearned" or "not seasoned enough" in the ways of Catholicism, especially within family life.

Gu gyo, a way of remembering and identifying individuals and the Korean Catholic Church throughout history, has its own historical amnesia. Although all Korean Catholics claim a lineage of the faith beginning with the martyrs of the early Korean Church, many claim today that a *gu gyo* household can usually only recall as far back as the Korean War. The period after the persecution of the early Korean church until the Korean War is often not recalled due to the inactivity and uneventful church life during this time. Many foreign missioners ministered in Korea during this period. However, not much has been reported by them or the natives. Church activity grew at a steady pace during this time; however, not until after the Korean War did the numbers of parishioners and clergy increase at an unprecedented rate. Thus, *gu gyo* links Koreans to their immediate Catholic family and the original Catholic lineage, but the decades in between signal an attitude toward periods of church history that is not upheld when heroic moments are absent.

The beginnings of Catholicism in Korea illustrate the difficult struggles of the Korean people in maintaining both their identity and faith. Figures such as the 103 martyrs, Andrew Taegon Kim in particular, were influential figures not only to the newly discovered faith but still today as Korean Catholics celebrate their first native priest as the exemplary model of the Korean faith. *Gu gyo* is another way of identifying oneself with the martyrs of old and the success of the church with its recent unprecedented growth. The uniqueness of the past and saintly figures such as the Korean martyrs are valued in Korea as ways of determining who Koreans are; simultaneously, this religious and ethnic self-identity has accompanied Korean immigrants in their migration process. However, an appreciation for and contribution of the Korean American Catholic experience is missing.

Today, Korean American Catholics watch their counterparts in Korea enjoy both social and ecclesial abundance as they struggle with their own faith and identity living in between two worlds. Struggles in the church and the world accompany any migrant group, and the same is true for Korean Americans. There are difficulties for Korean American Catholics in maintaining their Korean identity and Christian faith without an immigrant heritage in the Catholic Church that one can be proud of or call one's own. Immigrants and the next generation of Korean American Catholics cannot simply keep looking back to the historical events which have given meaning to Korean Catholicism; in order for Korean identity and Catholic faith to matter, an incorporation of past Catholic history of Korea with the more recent history of Korean Americans must come together. The difficult situations faced by many immigrants, especially in the ecclesial context, must be transformed into meaningful stories for the Korean American people. These immigrant stories of faith, as tragic and painful as they are at times, can become the vehicle for hope among subsequent generations just as the struggles of the faith in the early church in Korea propelled generations of believers.

CHAPTER 3

An Immigrant Narrative
Waves of Korean Immigration in U.S. History

Korean immigration to the U.S. has traditionally been categorized in three waves with a fourth emerging wave. Korean immigrants in the first wave (1903–1945) were laborers seeking economic refuge, picture brides seeking social refuge, and activists seeking political refuge. The second wave, known as the postwar period, lasted from 1945 to 1965. Korean immigrants during this time period sought relief from the ravages of the Second World War and Korean War. From 1965 to the present, the third wave has generally been categorized as the post-1965 immigration period. Many Koreans during this period left for the U.S. out of economic concerns and make up the majority of the Korean American population. Today, a fourth wave is emerging as transnational mobility increases due to corporate and government activities within a global economy. Those in the latter wave are quite different from their predecessors, as many come to the U.S. already educated, with vast resources and the reality of one day returning to Korea. Rather than systematically dividing the waves of immigration, an examination of the entire process of Korean immigration to the U.S. allows for common generational and cultural themes to arise, regardless of time periods, that is useful for both social and theological reflection of the Korean American journey.

Although there were a handful of Koreans who had made the journey to the U.S. prior to initial beginnings of Korean immigration in 1903, the need for laborers on Hawaiian sugar plantations became the real motivation that spurred noticeable immigration to the U.S. To attract Korean laborers to leave their homeland and come to the U.S., plantation owners looked to American missioners and their religious groups to promote Hawaii for its economic and religious possibilities.[1] "Religion

[1] Ronald Takaki, *Strangers from a Different Shore* (New York: Penguin Books, 1989), 53.

played an important role from the beginning, as recruiters for American companies called upon Protestant missionaries in Korea to persuade Koreans to immigrate to Hawaii to fill the need for plantation labor."[2] With Christianity playing such an important role in the beginnings of Korean immigration, most of these original immigrants to the U.S. were associated with the Protestant faith.

The Catholic Church in Korea had been recovering from the persecutions of the late nineteenth century during the initial immigration to the U.S. By this time, the French missioners were ministering to the Korean Catholic population and had no interest in promoting immigration to the U.S. In addition, the Catholic laity also shied away from political and social challenges such as immigration and stayed within their own sheltered but familiar surroundings. With Protestant missioners actively promoting immigration and economic progress through Western means, the Protestant churches became much more influential in Korea and throughout the diaspora. Thus, Korean Catholic influence in the U.S. parallels the church's influence in Korean society, which meant that the nonconfrontational and nonengaging attitudes with political and societal issues of the Korean Catholic Church would also limit their influence oversees. Not until the second half of the twentieth century did the Korean Catholic Church emerge in society once it embraced the social and political concerns of the nation. Once the Korean Catholic Church emerged from its own imposed sanctions, their ecclesial voice became a factor both in Korea and in the U.S.

In Hawaii, to keep both Japanese and Korean laborers content working on the plantations, picture brides were sent from Asia as early as 1910. Women as young as fourteen years old were matched by their physical appearance in their photos with laborers in Hawaii regardless of race and language. "Whereas the families of Japanese immigrants had arranged their children's picture-bride marriages, Korean migrants relied on Japanese agents to make the necessary arrangements for them. . . . At the time of their marriages, the men were generally twenty years older than their wives."[3] Along with these women seeking social and economic refuge were men seeking political asylum in the U.S. as Hawaii provided an environment distanced enough from Japanese retaliation but close enough to protest against Japanese imperialism. The 1919 Independence

---

[2] Sharon Kim, *A Faith of Our Own: Second-Generation Spirituality in Korean American Churches* (Piscataway, NJ: Rutgers University Press, 2010), 22.

[3] Takaki, *Strangers*, 56.

Movement of Korea forced some political activists to escape political persecution to continue their work in the U.S.

With the Protestant churches playing such a pivotal role in advancing immigration, religion became an important factor for some of the very first to call Hawaii their new home. Newly formed ethnic religious communities in Hawaii became the sociocultural and political hub, where the anti-Japanese occupation of Korea became one of the central rallying cries.[4] Protestantism with a patriotic consciousness did not resonate with the next generation as the geographic and cultural divide created new priorities for the offspring of these early immigrants. "It seems that the church's passionate and persistent preaching of Korean nationalism made it more or less irrelevant to these young people who did not share the same passion. Furthermore, the church also failed to provide a setting in which these young people could shield themselves from various effects of racism and discrimination."[5] Thus, the early church communities in Hawaii did not endure, as many found the church's social, political, and religious message not resonating with and adapting to the world confronting the next generation. Not until the third wave, the post-1965 immigration period, with the drastic rise of immigration to the U.S., would the remnants of the early Korean Protestant churches be restored along with the first seedlings of the Korean Catholic Church be planted.

The relevance of the early experience of church and society among Korean immigrants in Hawaii is yet to be fully realized. Without an in-depth investigation of the early Korean Christian communities and their connection to the brothers and sisters back home as well as their relationship with the next generation, we are able to glean only minor lessons for today's experience of immigration, church, and generational transitions. What the Hawaii experience reveals for Korean Americans is the need for a social and cultural hub, which the immigrant churches are able to provide. However, the political message that focuses solely on Korean nationalism fails to carry over to the next generation then and now. Whether it is the anti-Japanese campaign in the first half of the century or Korean nationalism during the second half, the next generation fails to embrace such sentiments as their concerns differ as the geographic and cultural divide widens. Therefore, the U.S. immigration experience

---

[4] Peter T. Cha, *The Role of a Korean-American Church in the Construction of Ethnic Identities among Second-Generation Korean Americans* (Ph.D. diss., Northwestern University, Evanston, IL, 2002), 8.

[5] Ibid., 9.

throughout history illustrates an ethnic group's need for a religious center incorporating cultural and political elements important to the immigrant generation but failing to resonant with the next generation. However, this failure does not mean that these religious communities are no longer valid for the next generation. Rather, the Korean American experience tells us that the need is perhaps even stronger as the struggle for identity in the retention of both heritages requires such a center based on religious beliefs. The challenge is not the survival of cultural religious communities but the message of relevance to the next generation as the future of these Korean American communities.

The formation of these cultural-political-religious hubs inevitably fails because of its evitable irrelevancy due to historic changes and lack of adaptation to the lives of subsequent generations. The situation in Hawaii is further heightened by the 1924 Immigration Act that bans further immigration. Without ongoing immigration supporting these ethnic hubs, the future is limited. Thus, there is a twofold lesson from this initial ecclesial experience in the early immigration to the U.S. On the one hand, Korean Americans require ethnic centers to formulate, acknowledge, and express their religious, social, cultural, and political well-being. On the other hand, these formulations and expressions do not endure with changing generational needs. This twofold lesson gleaned from the Hawaii experience is still relevant for us today. The difference today is the ongoing immigration that masks the limited future of the immigrant Korean Catholic communities. Unless the initial Christian communities are made relevant with the changing circumstances of the next generation, then these hubs preserving treasures of the Korean religious and cultural heritage will further exacerbate the *han* dilemma (dealt in the fourth chapter) as the immigrant groups fail in the transmission of what is important to them, while the next generation does not have the adequate resources to navigate their lives caught in between two worlds. Religious communities will endure, unlike their initial counterparts, because of ongoing immigration which continues the initial generation's model of church but fails to reinvent itself for subsequent generations.

In addition to the personal motivations for immigration, a communal sense emerged in the initial wave of immigration as the Korean government believed that more Koreans on U.S. soil would serve its own national interests. In addition, immigration in the beginning served as population control for Korea as portions of the peninsula struggled with intense poverty. Therefore, out of need for economic assistance and population concerns, the Korean government encouraged Koreans to emigrate, especially in the south. "Their emigration was encouraged, however, by a government which innocently hoped that, by doing so, it would somehow acquire a measure of prestige and support from the United States."[6]

Even with a carefully orchestrated emigration by Protestant missionaries and governmental effort on the Korean peninsula, certain world events could not be factored in. Out of fear and ignorance, the U.S. changed their immigration stance, banning further entrance by limiting or setting quotas for each country. Unfortunately, the rationale for limiting or banning certain people by their nation of origin was largely based on eugenic beliefs where preservation of the "superior" white race were on the forefront of people's mind in all sectors of society, including politicians and religious leaders. Thus, the National Origins Act or the Immigration Act of 1924 made Asian immigration to the U.S. illegal.

During the postwar period between 1945 and 1965, Korean immigrants first sought economic refuge in the U.S. after the Second World War. Japanese occupation during WWII left Korea barren and impoverished. With U.S. forces still in Asia to maintain peace while Japan was rebuilding after the devastation of war, about six thousand Korean immigrants made their journey to the U.S. In 1950, the Korean War furthered U.S. presence in the peninsula. The impoverished people of Korea in direct contact with U.S. servicemen provided another opportunity. This time, Korean women who married G.I.s, their offspring, and war orphans were allowed to make the U.S. their home. With the Korean peninsula at the center of wars and ideological conflict, Korean immigration was seen as a way of supporting U.S. global responsibilities.

> In terms of foreign policy considerations in the midst of the cold war, advocates for immigration reform argued that if the United States wished to portray itself as a leader of the "free world," the federal government had to eliminate racial discrimination not only in all domestic aspects of public life but also in its immigration policy. The act's supporters stressed that its implementation would benefit the United States by bringing in educated, skilled workers to fill labor needs in certain sectors of the economy, which was enjoying relative prosperity at the time. More importantly, organized labor, which had historically opposed immigration, decided to support the 1965 act because the United States Department of Labor would be given

[6] Lee Houchins and Chang-su Houchins, "The Korean Experience in America, 1903–1924," *Pacific Historical Review* 43, no. 4 (1974): 548.

full control over labor certification, which meant that no immigrant would be admitted under the occupational preference categories in industries that already had a sufficient number of American workers.[7]

The 1965 Immigration Reform Act removed years of prejudicial legislative barriers, allowing, among all ethnic groups, Korean families to immigrate to the U.S. in significant numbers. Thus, 1965 is a watershed year "marking the end of an ethnoreligious regime of European American Protestants, Catholics, and Jews and mostly Protestant African Americans."[8] With the lessening of quotas and restrictions, Koreans desired to reap the benefits of the U.S. while attempting to remain faithful to their ethnic heritage. Even with departure, displacement, and resettlement, Koreans were able to maintain this twofold desire of theirs mainly through their religious belief systems.

> Today, as in the past, people migrating to the United States bring their religions with them, and gathering religiously is one of the ways they make a life here. Their religious identities often (but not always) mean more to them away from home, in their diaspora, than they did before, and those identities undergo more or less modification as the years pass. To a greater or lesser extent, immigrants and their offspring adapt their religious institutions with religious communities already established here. The religious institutions they build, adapt, remodel, and adopt become worlds unto themselves, "congregations," where new relations among the members of the community—among men and women, parents and children, recent arrivals and those longer settled—are forged.[9]

The increase of Catholic presence in Korea directly and indirectly affected Korean Catholic immigrants. Directly, the emergence and maturation of the Korean Catholic Church translated into an increase of native clergy and religious, church leadership who also would influence the Catholic attitude in the diaspora. Indirectly, the rapid growth of the

---

[7] Min-Jung Kim, "Moments of Danger in the (Dis)continuous Relation of Korean Nationalism and Korean American Nationalism," *Positions* 5, no. 2 (1997): 371-72.

[8] R. Stephen Warner, "Introduction: Immigration and Religious Communities in the United States," in *Gatherings in Diaspora: Religious Communities and the New Immigration*, ed. R. Stephen Warner and Judith G. Wittner (Philadelphia: Temple University Press, 1998), 6.

[9] Ibid., 3.

Korean Catholic Church lessened the immigrant church experience throughout the diaspora. Once considered to be a political and economic resource to Korea, immigrants in the U.S. have not progressed at the same rate as their counterparts, most noticeably in church-related matters. Thus, the social, political, and ecclesial influence Korean immigrants once dreamed about exerting in their new homeland have been overshadowed by the economic prowess of Korea.

> Korean nationalism excludes Korean Americans/immigrants from a Korean national identity and fails to recognize them as a disenfranchised group within the United States who, in common with Koreans in the homeland, suffer the effects of the interconnecting histories of imperialism, capitalism, and racism. On the other hand, as immigrants incorporated as workers but not full-fledged citizen, Korean Americans construct an "ethnic" identity that alludes to the discursive forms of an earlier Korean "nationalist" identity; but while this construction of a collective national identity prepares the ground for challenging the racist state apparatus of the United States, the romanticism lurking beneath such an appropriation of national consciousness risks obscuring actual social and political realities in the homeland.[10]

An Immigration Metanarrative

Through the waves of immigration to the U.S., Koreans have created a metanarrative to explain their presence in a new country since many Korean Americans share a similar immigrant experience derived from the third wave. With the rise of new immigrants with resources and recent economic and social advances in Korea, immigrants who came in the late sixties all the way up to the nineties, along with their children, face increasing pressures to preserve their identities, the reasons for immigration, and their ongoing existence in the U.S. In order to understand the mind-set of this immigrant group, their use of metanarrative must be highlighted, especially in light of our eucharistic faith narrative, if it is to continue to serve in maintaining our identities as Korean Americans by shedding light on our current reality of being in between two cultures, languages, and peoples. "To preserve group identity despite diaspora, it is particularly important for 1.5-, second-, and third-generation Korean

---

[10] Kim, "Moments of Danger," 358.

Americans to (re)invent their ethnicity by invoking the homeland, at the risk, however, of romanticizing and distorting that history."[11]

Metanarratives are used to explain realities that cannot be simply said in common language. The unspoken nature of our lives is a complex reality, especially for Koreans. Due to the Confucian, Shamanic, and Buddhist influences in faith and society, there are many elements that are not permissible to address directly because of the dishonor and shame it brings upon the individual, family, and society. Thus, metanarratives are used to express core realities that cannot be verbalized. A common metanarrative, comprised of three components, can be attributed to the generation of Korean immigrants coming to the U.S. following the 1965 Immigration Act. The first component of the immigrant's metanarrative—their purpose for departure, displacement, and resettlement—arises from societal and economic circumstances. Koreans who immigrated to the U.S. in the late sixties and on will inevitably often point to widespread poverty after the Korean War. Largely based on economic reasons, many Korean immigrants came to the U.S. looking for a brighter future, one they could not envision in a poverty-stricken environment back home. A chance for an economically better life has always been a powerful motivating factor not only for Koreans but for most immigrants around the world. The second element of this metanarrative—their purpose for departure, displacement, and re-settlement—revolves around an external reality within the family but one that is intricately connected with the first: the education of their children.

Consistent to the rationale in the first metanarrative for a better life, Korean immigrants stressed education as the way for advancement. The strong Confucian stress on education in Korean culture along with limited societal and economical advancement in a new country caused many Korean immigrants to reason that all their struggles were for the betterment of their children. Thus, betterment came in two forms: money and education. The two were intertwined, especially in the immigrant group, as financial stability came from a good education since other means of attaining wealth were inaccessible due to the lack of linguistic, social, and technical skills in the initial immigrant group. Known for deferring their gratification, many initial immigrant groups deferred their own well-being for their children's future. This deferment leads us to the next component for departure, displacement, and resettlement. Without a larger vision, such deferments are not possible. Therefore,

[11] Ibid., 378.

Korean immigrants sought the release of their life's burden through the successes of their offspring. Rather than seeking peace through their own endeavors, Korean immigrants found an outlet of sorts by finding satisfaction through the events of their children.

Thus, the third factor of the Korean American immigrant metanarrative arises from internal discomfort and restlessness. Some Korean immigrants, especially those from the seventies and eighties, mention the smallness of Korea and the desire to live in a large country with wide-open spaces. The grandeur of the U.S. in geographic size and all her potential was a powerful attraction to Korean immigrants as a way of escaping their internal discomforts and limitations. Emblematically, the smallness and overpopulation in the major cities of South Korea reflected the internal constraints some Koreans felt after the Korean War and the widespread poverty of the country. Symbolically, the vastness of the U.S. appeared to truly be the land of opportunities, especially for releasing these internal constraints, since Korea is only slightly larger than the state of Indiana.

There are many more possible components to the metanarrative for Korean immigration after the 1965 Immigration Act; however, these three based on escaping widespread poverty, deferred gratification for their children's educational achievements, and internal reasons of discomfort and the desire to live in a larger country are the most commonly shared and visible within the Korean American community today with this generation of immigrants. Although these components comprised the metanarrative of immigration, a deeper reality still exists for departure, displacement, and resettlement.

What appears to be, at first glance, genuine and noble reasons for immigration are becoming shells of the Korean American experience. These three components making up the last generation's metanarrative for immigration have become acceptable ways of expressing the current situation of Koreans in the U.S. However, in reality, metanarratives speak very little to the history and identity unless the unspoken layer that this metanarrative addresses is not properly understood. More than ever Korean Americans are in need of the unspoken narrative to be told in order to understand their presence and purpose in between two worlds. Previously, the metanarratives did not need further explanations since Koreans in both the U.S. and Korea understood what it meant, having lived through common historical events, namely, the Korean War and widespread poverty. Today, the three components of this metanarrative no longer resonate with the initial immigrant group in the same manner or with the next generation. What is challenging the past expressions for departure, displacement, and resettlement is the emergence of Korean presence upon the global economy, the rapid rise in the standard of living for Korean citizens, the immense religiosity in Korea, and the current transnational movement of Koreans back and forth from their country of origin to their country of destination. The last on this list perhaps has challenged the metanarrative of the past the most.

Immigration today is vastly different from Asia in general and from Korea in particular than in previous times. Some Koreans making the journey across the Pacific are highly educated, have abundant resources, are already fluent in English, and are always in a mind-set to return back to their homeland. Immigration from other sectors of society is still occurring with the hopes of a better life in the U.S.; however, this new generation of highly skilled immigrants is challenging the previous reasons found in the Korean American metanarrative. For one thing, transnational migration is not necessarily for a better life in the U.S. but rather an opportunity to further one's position both socially, economically, and politically back in Korea. The journey to U.S. soil in this case is seen as a respite from the routine in Korea and as a stepping stone upon the return to their homeland. Thus, immigrants in this group do not refer to the components found in the previous metanarrative as their reason since they do not, in fact, permanently embrace their departure, displacement, and resettlement and see their current status as only a transitional one.

Transnational or transitional migration (for a lack of a better word) does not appeal to the poverty of Korea, the lack of educational opportunities, or the stuffiness of living in such a small country. Rather, the movement to another country is not seen as being caught between two worlds or cultures but an opportunity for betterment. The past metanarrative does not resonate with this group since they fondly look upon their return to Korea because the poverty and lack of opportunities are a distant memory. The overpopulation of major cities is no longer symbolic of internal constraints but is now a symbol of status with its high cost of living and trendsetting styles.

The challenge to the metanarrative of the past is due to its cultural and generational conditioning. Thus, the need to understand the unspoken reality for departure, displacement, and resettlement is vital to carry on the existence of Korean Americans today who mostly still trace their lineage to this metanarrative. Current transnational immigration has shattered some of the beliefs of the metanarrative, but the unspoken reality for immigration is still valid and true. Our identities as a people caught in between two worlds hinges on this understanding since it is our "creation" narrative of sorts because it tells the story of how we came into being. The metanarrative of the past was enough for immigrants after the Korean War and widespread poverty. However, their offspring need a narrative that will allow one to trace their lineage back to look forward. This is what is meant by being in between two worlds. The negative of this space is not having the narrative glasses to look back and, thus, not having the lens to look forward.

For a people dominated over the centuries by foreigners, Koreans maintained their identity and sanity by creating an image of a people known as *Dae-Han-Min-Guk* with uniqueness and purity. The idea of going oversees to another culture and people "violated" societal norms of *Dae-Han-Min-Guk*. However, out of economic, social, and personal necessity many made the journey to foreign lands. In addition, many who journeyed to different shores unknowingly were encouraged to do so by the Korean government for its survival and welfare. "More than any other Asian government, the South Korean government has actively promoted immigration as part of its population-control program. The Korean government recognizes that immigration contributes to economic stability. . . . Through its endorsement of immigration, as well as of capitalism, the South Korean government is thus complicit in the exploitation of the Korean American workers."[12]

Therefore, Korean immigration to the U.S. has played an important role in the development of Korea without the immigrants being formally recognized for their contributions in the development of a first-rate nation. On the one hand, the impoverished conditions in Korea led to its citizens departing their homeland for personal advancement and the betterment of Korean families and society. On the other hand, this departure was seen as a form of betrayal as the embrace of a foreign land somehow lessened one's Korean patriotism. Seen as siding with U.S. capitalistic and imperialistic tendencies, immigrants were stereotyped as greedy, materially motivated traitors by some.[13] Rather than acknowledging the necessity and the lack of opportunities that led to the departure from one's homeland and embrace of a foreign one or the moral and financial aid received from the diaspora communities benefitting Korea as a whole, the Korean psyche held a biased view of this overall experience. With the recent economic advancement of Korea, the diaspora support has become

12 Ibid., 372.
13 Ibid., 367–69.

unnecessary, therefore, leading to past contributions in the development of Korea as a global people and nation to be forgotten.

Although the U.S. is a country of immigration, living with immigrants is still a difficult reality for many Americans to truly embrace. As a positive, immigration is the cornerstone of our society. As a negative, immigrants today are different from their counterparts in the past, not because of language and culture (which we all share as immigrants), but because of skin color. This biological challenge to a country built on immigration is an unaddressed challenge in U.S. history and not always positively held in society because of the stark and contrasting differences in appearance. For Korean Americans to be able to do their share in answering this challenge, the metanarrative must also be connected to the unspoken narrative, one which was a given for the initial immigrant but one that now needs to be unearthed. To challenge the discrimination based on one's appearance requires a confident understanding of oneself. This can only arise with a complete narrative, proud of one's past in order to be proud of one's future. In so doing, we are able to restore the image of this country built upon immigrants in a positive light.

CHAPTER 4

Generations of *Han*

Basis of Korean American Identity, Immigration, and Religious Experience

As Korean Protestants begin to identify a Calvinistic-Confucian heritage, Korean Catholics must also begin to identify the Confucian, Buddhist, and Shamanic influences of their faith. It is a necessary enterprise to distinguish and identify the heritage of Korean American faith in order to fulfill Jesus' command of remembrance at the Last Supper. This is a difficult task on many levels. On the one hand, to distinguish what is authentically Christian and what is not is an impossible task since Christianity roots itself in specific locales, incorporating local customs into universal practices. On the other hand, Koreans are keenly selective in their memory because of the internal struggles of *han*. Foreigners have dominated Korea, and much suffering characterizes its history. Thus, Koreans find it extremely difficult to recall certain events in detail because of the shame and dishonor associated with it. Rather, only selective accounts in traumatic moments are recalled when they bring honor and captures the essence of how Koreans want to be remembered. A prime example of the way history is remembered in salvation history is the recollection of Andrew Taegon Kim as discussed in the earlier chapter on Korean Catholicism.

What further exacerbates the memory of Korean immigrants is the traumatic immigration experience consisting of departure, displacement, and resettlement. As illustrated in the last chapter, the explanation for the rupture of Korean lives resulting in an exodus is found in a metanarrative that attempts to resolve an external event, departure from Korea and the Korean people, with an internal existence, *han*. Korean Americans utilize a metanarrative to explain their current reality as immigrants through the collection of socially acceptable stories containing truth without having to reveal themselves in greater detail. These stories have become socially acceptable ways of expressing the tragedies of our lives without exposing individual dishonor or shame. However, the real-life situations and reasons for leaving behind the country and people became unspoken and seemingly forgotten, especially to the next generation. Thus, in order for the next generation to identify being both Korean and American, residing in the U.S. requires an understanding of our historical immigration process, beginning with the country of origin and continuing in the country of destination beyond "safe" metanarratives.

A metanarrative is the framework from which stories agreed upon by a community are told to explain their plight. Although a metanarrative historically carries a negative connotation, where the only or universal perspective was to be that of Europe's, we are making peace with it not as a singular view but rather as a way of connecting our local narratives with the metanarrative today. "[O]ur increasingly global situations demand stories that can describe and explain the worldwide interactions of diverse cultures and communities. From this convergence—a growing wariness of global stories coupled with situations which seem to demand them—has emerged a popular new double plot of world history in which cultural differentiation and cultural homogenization go hand in hand."[1] Through these stories, people from the beginning of time have expressed their beliefs, ideals, and understandings of the world through a common framework.

In many ways, a metanarrative continues the existence of a people in a somewhat folkloric fashion. There are many elements of truth involved in these local stories that make up the metanarrative. However, the sum of these stories does not encapsulate the entirety of an individual's lived experience or one's communal existence. The metanarrative of a group transcends time and space, for it speaks to many generations. In many ways, the stories comprising the metanarrative are familiar and identifiable since they follow a similar structure. Since the lived experience is much more than a common expression, a metanarrative cannot comprehend the entirety of one's being. Because the metanarrative is also being lived out as it explains our current state in life through the events of the past, it cannot be fully defined in one moment of time but continues to grow with the people who carry it. "So long as we are willing to refigure history, that sort of inclusiveness need not efface local experiences and

---

[1] Kerwin Lee Klein, "In Search of Narrative Mastery: Postmodernism and the People without History," *History and Theory* 34, no. 4 (1995): 275.

stories. Indeed, it may be the only way of taking seriously the voices, memories, and histories of others."[2]

Going beyond the first layers of the metanarrative reveals the complexity of Koreans and Korean Americans. The metanarrative speaks to the unspeakable reality within an individual, family, and society. Another way of expressing this reality for Koreans has been simply referred to as *han*. Within the Korean psyche influenced by Confucianism, Buddhism, Shamanism, and more recently a Judeo-Christian influence, *han* has been used to describe the inferiority and insecurities gripping the Korean people. There is no equivalent word in English for *han*, thereby making it even more difficult to express for the next generation. In short, *han* is the inexpressible anxiety, common to a people because of a shared experience of internal and external domination. "Han is an Asian, particularly Korean, term used to describe the depths of human suffering. Han is essentially untranslatable; even in Korean, its meaning is difficult to articulate."[3]

In his letter to the Romans, St. Paul mentions the inexpressible groanings within us that the Holy Spirit assists in lifting up in prayer. "In the same way, the Spirit too comes to the aid of our weakness; for we do not know how to pray as we ought, but the Spirit itself intercedes with inexpressible groanings. And the one who searches hearts knows what is the intention of the Spirit, because it intercedes for the holy ones according to God's will" (Rom 8:26-27, NAB). This inexpressible aspect of our lives is a part of our humanity since we know not how to pray and the Holy Spirit is given to all. However, to uncover this universal aspect, a particular understanding of the human person is necessary, as our inexpressible moments are also culturally conditioned.

For Koreans and Korean Americans, the inexpressible aspect of our lives is the historical, cultural, and social reality encompassed by *han*. This reality is perhaps quite appropriate to expound the hidden reality mentioned by St. Paul. *Han* encompasses multiple realities that are determined through differing perspectives. "Some authors translate it as a 'bitter feeling,' something directed inwards and arising from an unsatisfied or unfulfilled desire."[4] Others cast *han* as an inward pain or struggle

[2] Ibid., 298.
[3] Andrew Sung Park, *The Wounded Heart of God: The Asian Concept of Han and the Christian Doctrine of Sin* (Nashville, TN: Abingdon Press, 1993), 15.
[4] Mark C. Koo, *Conversion Experience in Korea: Gospel Insights of Forgiveness within the HAN Culture* (Ph.D. diss., Graduate Theological Union, Berkeley, CA, 2001), 14.

caused by displacement, the separation of where one is in life and where one wishes to be. Our broken humanity is realized in *han.*

> Han is the collapsed anguish of the heart due to psychosomatic, social, economic, political, and cultural repression and oppression. When internal and external forces cause our suffering to reach a critical point, it collapses to a singularity of agony. The collapsed sadness, bitterness, rage, and hopelessness become the vortex of our agony, overwhelming our conscious and unconscious modes of thinking. In other words, han is physical, mental, and spiritual response to a terrible wrong done to a person. It elicits a warped depth of pain, a visceral physical response, an intense rending of the soul, and a sense of helplessness.[5]

Along with the personal inexpressible dimension of *han*, a communal dimension exists as historical events and the cultural heritage of Korea perpetuate *han* where momentum is gained, thus compounding *han* with every generation. In particular, the invasion and oppression of foreign powers from the beginnings of Korea as a country and people up to recent times continue to impact the Korean people. Early on, "[b]esides the Mongols and the Manchus, there were the *Yŏjin* (Jurched), the *Koran* (Khitan), and the *Waegu* (Wäkö) invaders."[6] In the late nineteenth century, lasting until 1895, the war between China and Japan forced Korea in the middle of the East Asian conflict because of its location between the two rivaling powers. Just in the twentieth century alone, world events involving the Korean peninsula have left their indelible mark on the Korean people. Another disagreement between two powerful nations placed Korea in the midst of international conflict. This time, the war between Russia and Japan in 1905 was fought mainly in Korea because of its central location. The thirty-six years of Japanese occupation created a common oppressive history for the Korean people, deepening the shame-filled and unspoken reality of *han.* The Japanese occupation from 1910 to 1945 saw many Koreans being deported as slave laborers and sexual slaves to Manchuria, Siberia, and Japan. In addition, the separation of families and the nation after the Korean War in

---

[5] Andrew Sung Park, *From Hurt to Healing: A Theology of the Wounded* (Nashville, TN: Abingdon Press, 2004), 11.

[6] Elaine H. Kim, "Home Is Where the Han Is: A Korean American Perspective on the Los Angeles Upheavals," in *Reading Rodney King: Reading Urban Uprising*, ed. Robert Gooding-Williams (New York: Routledge, 1993), 218.

1953 continued the downward spiral of the Korean psyche overcome by despair and grief over the loss of loved ones. "One of the results of these cultural-annihilation policies was Koreans' fierce insistence on the sanctity of Korean national identity that persists to this day. In this context, it is not difficult to understand why nationalism has been the main refuge of Koreans and Korean Americans."[7]

Through a Korean culture and history filled with communal and personal domination, separation, and heartaches, Koreans have knowingly and unknowingly lived with *han* limiting their perspective of themselves and the world they live in. One way of explaining the large numbers of Korean immigration after the 1965 U.S. Immigration Act is through *han*. Without opportunities and resources, the release of *han* through personal and societal achievement and advancement was difficult. Immigrating to a land of opportunities was attractive for many families, particularly for their children, to help release the generational *han* through material and educational success in a new world. The parent group did not realize that the departure, displacement, and resettlement brought on by the immigration process would further complicate *han* within their own immigrant group as well as the next generation of Korean Americans. What is known as a postmemory *han* lingers even in immigrants who came at an early age or the subsequent generations with little or no knowledge of the Korea left behind. "Postmemory han is a paradox: the experience being remembered is at once virtual and real, secondhand and familiar, long ago and present. Such an enigma eludes straightforward representation, yet does not defy language altogether."[8]

Postmemory *han* explains how *han* is transmitted regardless of intention, location, or generations. This generational *han* has not been properly addressed by Korean Americans and the lack of knowledge identifying this condition creates further complications. What truly complicates the situation is that those who can remember do not and those who cannot remember desire to. "Korean immigrants tend to avoid discussing the experiences they survived, yet their experiences still haunt the second generation. What the children remember, moreover, is not generalized but vividly detailed and intimate."[9]

---

[7] Ibid., 230.

[8] Seo-Young Chu, "Science Fiction and Postmemory of Han in Contemporary Korean American Literature," *MELUS* 33, no. 4 (2008): 99.

[9] Ibid., 101–2.

Despite evidence that han is a medical condition, the illness remains difficult to categorize. . . . The answers are unclear. But if han is problematic, then postmemory han—the han that flows in the blood of Korean *Americans*—is infinitely more so. A second-generation Korean American might be haunted by her parents' anguish, but she would be equally haunted by the knowledge that she herself was not directly victimized by the circumstances that led to such pain. . . . To some extent, the answer lies in the power of the imagination to respond to historical narratives. Driven to understand the parents' world, the second-generation Korean American might ask them to tell stories about their childhoods.[10]

Using *han* to express the deeper reality of the Korean metanarrative for immigration sheds some light for Korean Americans and the work that is still needed for the next generation. *Han* as a key underlying element for immigration supplements the Korean metanarrative for departure of the country and people; however, it does not completely satisfy the unspoken reality. Grappling with *han* is a way of going deeper into the Korean American reality and bridging the separation and discontinuity caused by the clashing of two worlds. Because of Korea's occupation by foreign domination throughout centuries, a sense of inferiority has become part of the psyche as Koreans constantly compare themselves to others to affirm their well-being. This reality causing a lack of confidence and discontent within seeks release through various means. Typically, for a repressed group, recognition comes in the form of worldly success based on education, material wealth, and political and social status, whereby one feels superior to the other through modern means. The limited access and resources in Korea during the postwar period became a motivating factor for immigration to the United States where success appeared abundant in the land of opportunities, including an opportunity for releasing one's *han*.

Han, as a deeper reality of the metanarrative, has been rarely mentioned in public. One reason for this is that *han* is inexpressible. Another more relevant rationale is that *han* for many Korean Americans has not been released and has only transformed itself in the initial immigrant group and in the next generation. Many Korean immigrants who pursued the "American Dream" were never able to release their personal *han*. Because of the nature of *han*, a constant comparison to others becomes

[10] Ibid., 98.

inherent for one's well-being for Korean Americans who have never been able to define success other than through the experiences of their native homeland. The immigration experience has shown that the Korean standards of measurement in personal achievement and in society do not easily translate to the immigrant group and subsequent generations.

While Korean Americans use comparisons with others as a motivating source in their personal lives as well as to get ahead in society, these comparisons also perpetuate the cyclical dilemma of *han*. By comparing one's life, career, education, material wealth, and even one's children with another's, Korean Americans continuously strive for much more and never enjoy and appreciate their accomplishments along the way. The reason for this is that comparisons reveal that someone else is always on top. Through the comparison of one's state in life to others, no rest can be found for the weary as there are always more mountains to climb, more feats to accomplish, and more personal disciplining to achieve. Since the next generation of Korean Americans does not have their own moral and social measurements incorporating the influences of both worlds that give them their identity, they also perpetuate the cyclical dilemma of *han* as their only guide is to inherit their initial immigrant mentality for success. Thus, success is realized when one is at the very top with no comparisons to be made. There is, however, a lack of satisfaction in every accomplishment achieved as Korean Americans continually strive to calm their interior restlessness and insecurities as well as the external voices from their parents and the Korean community. Unable to achieve the ultimate pinnacle in any field, many immigrants never reach a level of success and security where they are able to speak confidently about the struggles of their existence, especially in Korea, and the real reasons for departure, displacement, and resettlement.

As a majority of Korean Americans professes a Judeo-Christian belief, the importance of comparing one's life also becomes evident in one's faith. Rather than being at peace in one's relationship with God, restlessness overwhelms believers as they always feel that more can be achieved or accomplished to increase one's faith life. Thus, spiritual life is not immune to *han* as an unsettled existence permeates all areas of the Korean American person. Korean Americans naturally strive for more in society because of the ongoing comparisons of their lives; thus, this drive unquestionably flows over to their faith life. For some, this will and determination are seen as Christian gifts of Korean Americans to the rest of the world. Through hard work, dedication, and commitment, Korean Americans find their faith to be *par excellence* over other ethnicities who profess a similar belief.[11] Without questioning the motivating factors behind their spiritual lives, Korean Americans see their efforts in both church and society as a positive and an exemplary model for all to emulate. However, the internal discontent still resides in Korean Americans regardless of what is achieved because of the ongoing comparisons of one's life to the other who is more accomplished, better educated, and financially well off.

For the initial Korean Catholic immigrants, the Legion of Mary, or *Legio Maria* or simply *Legio*, as it is more commonly referred to in Korean, is a very popular devotion as it was in the United States back in the fifties and sixties for Euro-Americans. Part of the attraction to this type of prayer is that it fits well into the Korean immigrant psyche, but not necessarily to the next generation of Korean American Catholics. As the name of the devotion reflects, a militaristic model outlining one's prayer life consisting of rosaries and service is demanded. Being told how to pray and act in church and the world becomes a powerful measuring stick, especially in an environment that is unfamiliar and difficult to navigate. Thus, a majority of Korean Catholic immigrants belong to *Legio* groups attending weekly meetings. During their prayer meetings, each member must report how many times rosaries and Masses were offered. In addition, the number of times or hours spent in service is also detailed. Several things are accomplished during the reports of the *Legio* meetings. First, there are validations for *Legio* members of how well or poorly someone walked with the Lord since the last meeting as the small group dynamic offers comparison without too much public shame or dishonor. Second, accountability through formal reporting in this group dynamic motivates the immigrant group to strive for more spiritually. Finally, the small-group community found within the *Legio* group gives the laity a sense of church membership and participation in the larger parish community.

Ongoing Comparisons, Ongoing *Han*

Even if a Korean lifts himself or herself out of poverty and becomes successful, there are lingering effects. For example, if a person of meager beginnings in Korea becomes economically successful and graduates from Korea's most prestigious university, this pedigree is not enough to release

[11] Pyong Gap Min, *Preserving Ethnicity through Religion in America: Korean Protestants and Indian Hindus across Generations* (New York: New York University Press, 2010), 141–42.

the *han* one is struggling with. This is because there are always others with similar credentials but perhaps with a more prestigious family lineage of education and wealth. Due to Koreans' inability for self-contentment as they are always in comparison with others, the person dealing with his or her *han* struggles to feel accomplished and satisfied even when personal goals are achieved. Thus, a reason for this immigration is to come to the U.S. and embrace a lower socioeconomic status in the hopes that his or her offspring can become even more successful. If the next generation of Korean American succeeds educationally by attending another prestigious university such as Harvard, then the purpose for immigration has been achieved. The releasing of *han* for the older immigrant group is obtained because now there is a family lineage that rivals most others. *Han* is now released even though the person who was successful in his own right in Korea but continually felt inferior because of others can finally say that his or her family tree is "more successful" due to elements that cannot be found in the other's situation. Sadly, this is not the case for many Korean immigrants and their offspring because of the ambiguous and undefined levels of success and satisfaction within the immigrant experience. Currently, the only guide for success that Koreans Americans can conceptualize is the pinnacle levels of society: the most prestigious schools, the best socially acceptable careers, and greatest financial well-being, all of which perpetuate and exacerbate the cyclical dilemma of *han*.

Although *han* further deepens our understanding of the Korean American metanarrative for immigration, it still does not express the core reality. In many ways, *han* is a deeper revelation but still a very generic expression. Going deeper means the coherent or incoherent verbalization of the specific *han* within an individual, especially in the discussion of immigration. Today, *han* appears in the backdrop of discussions but does not have a significant place in our storytelling. One reason for this lack of appropriation of *han* in the immigrant metanarrative is its inexpressible character. Another rationale is that *han* touches the unspoken core realities too closely. The challenge is to allow the initial immigrant group to remember their narratives without the scrutiny of inferiority and shame. Waiting for a day when family success will magically transform our self-worth in order to tell our narratives is a fallacy that haunts Korean Americans.

CHAPTER 5

Beginnings of the Immigrant Church in the 1970s and 1980s

Catholics of Korean American descent not only share a common immigration history of the 1970s and 1980s but their stories of growing up in Catholic immigrant communities resonate with one another because of their similarities as immigrants locating their culture and faith in a safe haven. Many Korean religious communities in the U.S. began in the 1970s and 1980s in small groups as displaced immigrants felt the need for communal support. Within these small groups, meetings sometimes took place in people's homes or in borrowed space from the English-speaking church. Just as Korean immigrants had to squeeze their way into society to stake a claim in it, the ecclesial landscape posed a similar challenge. As these small groups gained membership and recognition through their participation in the English-speaking liturgies while holding their own meetings in Korean, they soon gained the attention of parochial and diocesan leadership.

Unable to properly engage them pastorally because of linguistic and cultural differences, parishes and dioceses, along with the newly forming communities, sought assistance from Korean priests available for work in the United States or from religious missioners after their missionary service in Korea. Unlike the European immigration experience in the early 1900s, native clergy were not originally sent along with the immigrants. The Korean bishops did not initiate such a pastoral plan for the care of their people in the diaspora because of their own growing pains back home. Many dioceses focused on nurturing native vocations in the hopes of replacing foreign missioners to meet the needs of the growing Catholic population. The common beginnings of these immigrant communities in the 1970s and 1980s thus include forming lay leaders first gathering in small groups, then inviting outside priestly leadership either from English-speaking priests willing to work with these communities even without the proper linguistic skills, from missioners returning from Korea upon the completion of their assignments, or from Korean priests (e.g., those studying abroad) with visas allowing them to work in forming the first communities. Through the self-sacrifice of parishioners and clergy, the Korean immigrant experience of Catholicism began to flourish throughout the U.S. The following examples highlight some of the developments of these early communities and will resonate with many who grew up with the beginnings of these immigrant communities.

Early Priestly Presence

Fr. Richard Parle or *Cha Shinbunim* (*Cha* is taken from the second syllable of Richard as pronounced by Koreans; *Shinbunim* is the transliteration of the Korean term for "Father"), as he is affectionately called within the Korean American communities in the Pacific Northwest, began his priestly ministry in Korea as a Colomban missioner right out of the seminary. Life near the Korean demilitarized zone (DMZ) dividing the north and the south after the Korean War was not without its challenges, especially with widespread poverty throughout the country. It was in these harsh and unstable times that this young Colomban father had to quickly learn to incorporate the sacramental life with the Korean people's struggles. During his three assignments lasting fifteen years as an overseas missioner, Fr. Parle helped in rebuilding the local parish communities as well as their dioceses as the Catholic Church in Korea underwent a rebuilding period similar to the lives of the Korean people after the devastating civil war.

The fifteen years of living through the hot, humid summers and bitter, cold winters near the DMZ formed the necessary skills for the future of this missioner vocation. Not only would his comprehension of the Korean language continue to serve him well journeying with the Korean immigrants back home, but his sense of mission developed in Korea became just as vital. Once his assignment in Korea was completed, Fr. Parle returned to the states to discern his next area of ministry. Joining his community in the Seattle, Washington, area eventually opened doors in working with the Korean people again, this time establishing several Catholic communities for Korean immigrants throughout the Northwest. In the mid-seventies, Fr. Parle was asked to celebrate a Korean liturgy at the cathedral requested by the parishioners and archdiocese. What began as a monthly liturgy quickly grew into weekly gatherings as news of the Korean Mass spread throughout the greater Seattle area. The Seattle-based Korean American community rooted themselves as a permanent fixture in the ecclesial landscape of the archdiocese as they began to gather at a nearby parish in 1976. St. Edward's parish provided temporary space until the newly formed community was invited to a more stable environment at St. George, located just south of the downtown area.

Shortly after the formation of the Seattle area community, Korean immigrants in the south began to form their own community as well. Soon, Fr. Parle traveled to Tacoma, Washington, on Sunday afternoons to celebrate the sacraments after he had finished the Korean liturgy in Seattle. Sts. Peter and Paul became the first site where an afternoon Mass formed the beginnings of the faith and cultural lives of the people of the Tacoma area. If celebrating two Masses were not enough with two entirely different communities separated by an hour and a half drive, the people of Portland, Oregon, requested Fr. Parle visit them for their sacramental needs as well. Throughout the 1980s, Fr. Parle was not only in full-time ministry to Koreans in the greater Seattle area but now the priestly figure throughout the Northwest. The missionary zeal of going to Korea and serving in some of the harshest conditions allowed this faithful servant to travel many miles celebrating the sacraments in Seattle on Sunday mornings, Tacoma on Sunday afternoons, and Portland on a Sunday evening once a month at the motherhouse of the Holy Names Sisters. And when this Pacific Northwest missioner had extra time, he would go to a tiny mission community near Olympia, Washington, to minister to the dispersed Korean immigrants there. Through his unrelenting dedication to the Korean immigrants, especially in their infant and displaced faith communities, Fr. Parle laid the groundwork for the Korean people to realize portions of their "American Dream." He did this by establishing faith communities throughout the I-5 corridor spanning from the Canadian border down to Oregon. Today, the Korean American Catholic centers of Seattle, Tacoma, and Portland are all staffed with priests from Korea and are a vibrant part of the faith journey of people of Korean descent in the Pacific Northwest.

Not all beginnings of the Korean immigrant faith community have such heroic figures. Other communities were built on the sweat and labor of many who are often forgotten by the recent immigrants. Their sweat, labor, and love for starting the ethnic religious community equaled that of their energies in caring for their own families. Many volunteers joyfully embraced long nights and weekends at church after spending long hours at work. Without their time, effort, and dedication, the newly gathered communities would scarcely have had a chance. Although many immigrants during the 1970s and 1980s were self-employed laborers, they were not unskilled, for many were professionals or had acquired abilities back in their homelands that were invaluable in establishing social and religious groups.

Many immigrant churches were established with the help of former missioners who worked in Korea. Others were created with the assistance of Korean priests who were sent by their bishops in Korea to minister in the diaspora or by clergy studying abroad who took the initiative to temporarily assist these infant communities. Those lucky enough to be assigned a priest as if they were an extension of the Korean diocese had a dedicated full-time pastor who initially related well to the mentality of the initial immigrant group since they also just recently left Korea themselves. Having a spiritual leader who was similar to them in many ways reassured these Catholic immigrants in their decision for departure, displacement, and resettlement. Feeling like they were able to re-create something that was culturally and religiously familiar in an unfamiliar environment meant the preservation of the two most important things to this ethnic group: faith and culture. However, the temporary assignments of Korean clergy did not necessarily reflect the immigrants' need and experience as permanent settlers, thus plaguing the establishment and development of some communities still to this day.

The latter group who had to rely on temporary pastoral care struggled until they were able to receive the pastoral attention from a full-time priest from Korea. Most diaspora communities of Korean descent were not able to receive pastoral care by a native Korean-speaking priest until Korean vocations flourished and reached unprecedented heights in the 1990s and 2000s. Prior to the plethora of Korean clergy, immigrant communities in the U.S. sought pastoral care from other resources. One source of pastoral care came from non-Korean Catholic priests celebrating liturgies in English while the parishioners responded in Korean. Immigrant communities also found clergy support by inquiring into temporary assistance from Korean priests studying abroad. For example, during their summer breaks, Korean priests studying in Rome or in the U.S. provided sacramental care to the immigrant communities. It was mutually beneficial as the Korean clergy were able to earn much-needed money for their studies while the infant faith groups received the much-needed attention not only for their spiritual needs but for social and psychological care arising from the immigration experience. In many ways, the coming together and building of the immigrant church was symbolic of their hope and future.

Ministry to the Korean immigrant group in the 1970s and 1980s was a first in many ways. Although Koreans previously departed their homelands, the numbers were either not large enough or Korea was not in a position to take care of their own outside their national borders. Korean immigration to the U.S. after the 1965 Immigration Act provided an opportunity for immigrants to creatively find solutions to address their multiple and complex needs. Eventually, the economic and social rise of Korea in the new millennium provided resources previously unavailable for those living in the diaspora, especially in terms of Korean clergy presence. Today, it is not uncommon to find Korean communities in the U.S. with two native Korean priests. Along with the increase in priestly presence, many religious sisters came to minister to the Korean-speaking immigrant groups as well. The natural inclination for Korean-speaking clergy because of their own plight had its drawbacks as the younger generation often did not receive adequate pastoral care. The social, cultural, and religious spaces carved out in the U.S. regulated many offspring who were not fluent in Korean or well versed in the culture to observe the faith life of their parents from a distance rather than as main congregational participants and contributors.

As a creative measure to address some of the pastoral concerns of this ethnic group, deacons were ordained to serve some of the immigrant communities. Today, we are accustomed to seeing deacons in both English- and Korean-speaking ministries. However, the first Korean immigrants ordained to the permanent diaconate in the 1980s became a groundbreaking occasion in the history of the local and universal church. When the French missioners arrived in Korea in the eighteenth century, the permanent diaconate was for most practical purposes a forgotten ministerial position. Considered more as one of the steps toward priesthood, the diaconate was not utilized as priestly ministry was upheld and Europe did not suffer from a lack of vocation at the time. It was not until the Second Vatican Council in the 1960s that the Catholic Church rediscovered and appropriated proper ministerial space for the permanent diaconate. Benefitting from the implementation of the permanent diaconate, several Korean immigrants entered their local diocesan programs and were eventually ordained deacons to serve the immigrant communities. Deacons assisted the priests from Korea or supplying Korean linguistic help to the non-native Korean priests providing temporary assistance. The diaconate rose out of a shortage of clergy, regardless of ethnicity. However, the Catholic Church in Korea has never fully embraced the permanent diaconate. In light of the overwhelming numbers of vocations in Korea, it is not likely that the permanent diaconate will regain its place in the Korean ecclesial landscape as it has in the diaspora.

Shortly after Korean Americans began entering the diaconate program, the younger generation of the initial immigrant group also started to enter the seminary. Today, Korean American vocations to the priesthood are very small in numbers compared to their counterparts in Korea, but their impact and need are great, especially for subsequent generations. Within the presbyterate are generational, cultural, and linguistic issues reflecting the overall Korean American Catholic population. Some are more fluent in Korean than English, more knowledgeable in Korean customs than the American way of life, more comfortable in a monoethnic environment, and vice versa. However, regardless of cultural and linguistic comfort levels, ordained priests of Korean descent have responded to their calling to address the needs of the immigrant community and the next generation. This is a need that is usually experienced firsthand growing up in these communities.

As previously noted, many Korean religious women went overseas to address some of the immigrants' spiritual concerns. Similar to the priests who usually served a four-year assignment before returning to Korea, women religious working in the parishes rotated. However, recently, the Sisters of the Korean Martyrs created a new province which includes both the U.S. and Mexico. While provinces including the U.S. in conjunction with provinces in Korea have been created previously, this creation was a unique departure from the previous models of Korean ministry abroad. Rather than simply working for a limited period of time in the U.S. and then returning home, the Sisters of the Korean Martyrs are working toward full immigration and naturalization. The decision to select this province is a life-changing event, as these religious women are deciding to live out the rest of their lives and ministries in North America. The initial transition to an independent province from Korea has had mixed results. Some sisters have embraced their new hyphenated identities now belonging to two worlds as immigrants, especially the missioners in Mexico. Some have experienced the isolated realities of living as a minority in a foreign land and have returned to Korea. However, this "experiment" to create an independent province that will one day hopefully be self-sustaining economically and vocationally has its merits. By doing so, the commitment to the immigrant church is more than one of lip service. These religious women have a vested interest in the ecclesial, social, and cultural success of the Korean American people now that they have joined their ranks.

The creation of a North American province for a Korean religious community reveals the state of immigration today. In particular, the recent move by the Sisters of the Korean Martyrs in their noble cause to live with those finding their way in the diaspora highlights the similarities and differences between the immigrants of the 1970s and 1980s and of those today. When Koreans came in large numbers after the 1965 U.S. Immigration Act, many left Korea with the intention that they would never return to the homeland. This outlook of never returning differs significantly from the Latin American migrants who intend to return to their pueblos even after their death. The "total" departure from Korea forced many to make the U.S. their home, even when disillusioned by the reality of life striving for the "American Dream." Today, the experience of immigration reveals that the reasons for departing Korea still remain true today as well as being unspoken. Many religious women who chose to live out their lives in North America came because of family already in the U.S. or through their own restlessness or *han*, which at first appeared to diminish with the missionary adventures of going overseas. However, the reality of the U.S. and Mexico, in particular, the isolated parish existence, including cultural differences between generational immigrants, and the sometimes paralyzing social status living as a minority, can be overwhelming to some.

After brief attempts at living abroad as a permanent immigrant, some religious women have returned to a life of familiarity in Korea. The difference today is not the reasons for leaving Korea or the intention of becoming a permanent citizen in the diaspora. The difference is that immigrants like these religious women have personal or institutional resources and support to return to Korea and resume their lives, an opportunity that was previously never afforded. Because the previous generation of immigrants did not have this luxury, they adapted their lives in order to survive in their new land. Part of this survival was to re-create something important and familiar to them, a community of faith. The luxury of returning to Korea keeps new immigrants from overcoming their hurdles to make the best of their opportunities, only to return where the release of *han* sought through the immigration experience intensifies.

CHAPTER 6

Pastoral Challenges

The pastoral challenges for Korean American Catholics are numerous and becoming more complicated with ongoing immigration from Korea along with the maturation of the next generation. Pastoral sensitivity is needed in multiple areas, ranging from ecclesial and spirituality concerns along with the formation of both cultural and generational bridges in order for identity formation in successive generations. As noted in chapter 4, *han* plaguing Koreans and Korean Americans creates an unhealthy environment where comparisons are constantly being made. From grades to language proficiency to dress, people of Korean descent are constantly being measured to one another without any solace in sight. Thus, being in comparison to not only Koreans and others like them, Korean Americans are also subjected to being compared with other ethnic groups that dominate the societal and ecclesial landscape. The comparing of one's own religious community in the U.S. to the Catholic Churches in Korea, to English-speaking Catholic communities, and especially to Korean American Protestant churches puts the next generation of Korean American Catholics at a substantial disadvantage.

The constant comparisons between the Catholic Church in Korea means immigrant Catholic communities in the U.S. will always be considered inferior to their Korean counterparts. With the phenomenal economic and ecclesial growth in recent years, the Korean Catholic Church dwarfs the sister communities in the U.S. In the mid-1970s, when many of today's Korean immigrants came to the U.S., the Korean Catholic Church reached a million members. Today, there are over five million Catholics throughout South Korea. Although Catholics in Korea or in the U.S. represent roughly 10 percent of the total population (a little more in Korea and a little less in the U.S.), the sizable presence of Catholics in the southern half of the Korean peninsula allows the Korean Catholic Church to be a vibrant influence in both the religious and political domains, whereas a tenth of the total immigrant population in the U.S.

translates to roughly a hundred thousand Korean American Catholics. Today, the total Korean American Catholic population rivals that of the Catholic population in Korea in the 1930s.

Comparing current church activities of Korean American Catholic communities, some located in very rural areas across the United States, to their counterparts in Korea, where the Catholic Church is enjoying unprecedented numbers in the growth of priests, laity, and church activities, means that Catholics living in the diaspora will continue to be unsettled in their spiritual lives. This comparison between Catholic populations is fueled by two sources. The first source was created when Koreans endured departure, displacement, and resettlement, seeking betterment in all areas of their lives. The belief system which immigrants carried with them founded a church in the diaspora that represents not only their beliefs but also their culture, ethnicity, and identity. Thus, to have an "inferior church" that is being lived out in constant comparisons means that the betterment sought by the initial Korean immigrant group never has the opportunity to be realized.

The second source of constant comparisons is through the ongoing immigration of Koreans, in particular, visiting Catholic priests and religious sisters who come to minister for roughly four years and then return to Korea. By coming as temporary missioners, Korean priests and sisters do not invest in the future realities of immigrants, especially when it comes to the next generation, where Korean ethnicity and language become foreign. The temporary mentality of these modern-day missioners creates an environment where the Korean Catholic Church becomes the model for all spiritual activities without ever considering the contributions of Korean Americans through the immigrant and resettlement experience. The difficulty with this perspective is that as time goes on, some Korean practices become unfamiliar as well as unattainable because of limitations in material and human resources. In addition, the narrow mind-set that all ministries must not only look similar to those in Korea but resemble the church life of the diocese where the missioners originated from also burdens immigrant Catholics and the next generation, limiting their ability to identify their own unique contributions to the local church as well as hindering their development as a Catholic community similar yet different from that of the Korean experience because of immigration.

Ongoing immigration is a definite cause of tension between the initial immigrants who built most of the Korean Catholic Churches in the U.S. and with recent immigrants who have a lesser vested interest in the actual building structure. One of the reasons often cited for building an ethnic religious community was primarily to pass on the faith to their offspring, the next generation. This has yet to materialize. The ongoing influx of new immigrants from Korea, along with recent missioners, places the main ministerial focus still on the immigrant groups with Korean as their primary language as well as maintaining familiarities recently left behind. "For the first generation, the immigrant congregation is a home away from home, a remembrance of Zion in the midst of Babylon, but precisely because of this, the congregation can feel oppressive to an inevitably Americanizing second generation."[1] Thus, tensions between newcomers and forerunners add to the challenges of the ethnic religious communities by adding to the generational layers not only between the first and the second but also between initial first generation and their recent counterpart.

The Korean mind-set further fuels a Korean "isolationist and elitist attitude" toward not only their own people but also the rest of the world. With the recent social, political, and economic advancement in South Korea, many Koreans wonder why others cannot develop in a similar manner. From their perspective, dedication, hard work, and faith are the only things needed if success is to be attained. The lack of success is then attributed to the lack of hard work of an individual or people. On the one hand, this drive propels many to strive for more, especially in the church where Catholics seek to make their house of God "better" than others. On the other hand, this drive for success in all areas of life is environmentally conditioned where, without proper resources and guidance, all the hard work and energy will not produce the desired effects. The Korean mind-set often neglects this aspect where the environmental conditions along with such dedication are required to achieve the desired outcome.

In one sense, Korean American Catholics are very modern. The desire to build their own ethnic church adds to the ecclesial landscape of local dioceses. However, the limited population numbers hinder Korean Catholic immigrant communities and subsequent generations from achieving a significant impact beyond their own enclave. Therefore, English-speaking communities never are afforded an opportunity to learn about their brothers and sisters in faith as well as receiving a

---

[1] R. Stephen Warner, "Introduction: Immigration and Religious Communities in the United States," in *Gatherings in Diaspora: Religious Communities and the New Immigration*, ed. R. Stephen Warner and Judith G. Wittner (Philadelphia: Temple University Press, 1998), 25.

valuable contribution of a local church experience. Because of the lack of connection and encounter between Korean American Catholics and their English-speaking counterparts, their immigrant church experience is lumped into similar categories with other Asian immigrants who came to the U.S. with their belief systems or as a "generic" immigrant group who should follow the same patterns of societal and ecclesial assimilation as those of the European immigrants in the early 1900s. However, the present immigration of multiple non-European groups reveals they are phenotypically different and that the "white American" assimilation is not an attainable reality since the context of immigration from the country of origin as well as the context of the country of destination is unique for each non-European immigrant.[2]

> If there was ever a linear process by which immigrants assimilated to American culture, it no longer exists. If in the past immigrants (or more likely their children) first became ethnics and later plain Americans, today the picture is more complex. . . . [T]here is no longer just one "America" that newcomers enter nor only one "American identity" that they may adopt. Newcomers encounter a pluralistic social context rich with types and categories to which they may be assigned.[3]

Being considered centers or missions rather than parishes by dioceses throughout the U.S. hampers the development of Korean American Catholic communities as well. One rationale for limiting the juridical distinction of ethnic enclave stems from the U.S. Catholic Church's experience of European immigration, where national parishes were established. German, Polish, Italian, and other European churches were created literally blocks from each other as each immigrant group was accompanied by their own clergy. Eventually, the common English language, along with the fair skin of each ethnic group, fostered a community beyond ethnic lines. Thus, national parishes were no longer needed, and the closure of these ethnic centers traumatized many clinging to their heritage. With such a backdrop, many church leaders steered clear of creating new national parishes. Fearing similar outcomes where ethnic parishes would have to be closed after the next generation learned English, many dioceses decided to wait out the current situations of Asian immigrants in the

---

[2] Ibid., 12.
[3] Ibid., 18.

Catholic Church in the hopes that, by the next generation, the need for such ethnic religious centers would no longer exist. However, in the process of waiting for the future, many dioceses have failed to acknowledge the Korean immigrant church as authentic expressions of church as well as seeking their contribution to a society and church built on a unique modern immigration experience.

Finally, immigrants and the next generation of Korean American Catholics fall into the comparison trap once again. This time, comparisons between Catholic and Protestant immigrant churches, especially in their outreach ministries to youth and young adults, are noticeable. Comparisons in the Korean culture occur when there is a dominant presence that reminds Koreans of their shortcomings. First, comparisons to the abundant Korean Catholic Church enjoying immense growth could not be avoided because of the Korean heritage of the people in the pews along with the Korean mind-set of missioners. Next, comparisons to the dominant English-speaking Catholic Church became evident as even the hierarchy dismissed the uniqueness of this authentic expression of the local church. Last but not least, the Protestant churches dominate the landscape of Judeo-Christianity here and abroad. Unlike in Korea, Protestants enjoy a prominent presence encapsulating a majority of the entire Korean American population. Not all immigrants are Protestant when they depart from Korea but many become so after the shock of displacement and the difficulties of resettlement as Protestant congregations provide a refuge where a familiar lifestyle, language, culture, and opportunities become visible, for these are not clearly identified in the host country.

In the 2000 U.S. census, there were approximately three thousand churches embraced by the Protestant majority. With eight times the number of people and resources than Korean American Catholics, Korean American Protestants are able to create active communities and programs, especially for the next generation. From academia to pastoral ministries focused primarily on the next generation English speakers, Protestants have a huge advantage over Catholics due to their large presence. In addition, most Protestant ministers are immigrants themselves. Rather than coming to the United States as a temporary missioner like their Catholic counterparts, Protestant ministers migrate with their people with the intent to live out the rest of their lives in a similar fashion as their congregation. Today, with such numbers, especially those influenced by English-speaking Evangelicals, second-generation ministers focus primarily on the work with the next generation who are not only visible but also the civic and spiritual leaders of their people.

Due to similar experiences of immigration as well as family and church life in the resettlement process, Korean American Protestants are suitable dialogue partners regarding the resettlement experiences with their Catholic counterparts. The vast numbers of Korean American Protestants have allowed for exploration and experimentation of the next generation. Researchers and scholars have been able not only to identify family, pastoral, and social issues of Korean American Protestants but also to witness the numerous second-generation English-speaking pastors who are able to provide creative ministries often unavailable within Catholic circles. Although not all experiences are transferrable due to doctrinal delineations, however, much of the social and cultural issues in the religious sphere are relatable.

In 2007, the Lilly Foundation sponsored research and writing for the development of a Korean American religion and spirituality.[4] Protestant writers dominated the final text, and the lack of Catholic contribution reflects the pastoral and academic underdevelopment in Korean American Catholicism. Because of the dearth of written reflection on the Korean American Catholic experience, some of the challenges faced by Korean American Protestants can begin the necessary conversations for Catholics.

Most importantly, the Korean American Protestant experience can assist Catholics in exploring the generational issues within the ecclesial context. Tensions between the immigrant group and the next generation are both real and common, regardless of denomination affiliation, for many in the immigrant generation stress the importance of maintaining cultural values as well as religious ones. By creating a religious environment similar to those found in their homeland, Korean American Protestants are able to maintain their cultural values that support ethnic ideals such as filial piety, language maintenance, and ethnic preservation.[5] Tensions arise since the next generation of Korean American Protestants desire to minimize "Korean cultural components" and stress Christian values that they see as universal.[6] There are two problems created in this standoff between immigrant cultural churches and so-called next generation universal Christian-focused churches. For one, this situation

---

[4] David Yoon and Ruth Chung, *Religion and Spirituality in Korean America* (Champaign: University of Illinois Press, 2008).

[5] Pyong Gap Min, *Preserving Ethnicity through Religion in America: Korean Protestants and Indian Hindus across Generations* (New York: New York University Press, 2010), 177.

[6] Ibid.

poses two extremes with no middle ground and, thus, culture becomes an either-or proposition. The other critical issue is the narrowness of second-generation insistence on "non-cultural" infused beliefs, which brings us to the Korean American Protestant experience of young adults, shedding further insights into the necessity of culture and faith.

Evangelical influences on Korean Americans on college campuses are changing the religious and cultural landscape of this ethnic group. During their college years, Korean Americans are open to both academic and religious learning. Religious groups on college campuses involving both Euro-American and Korean American English-speaking outreach ministries reformulate a belief system where Korean culture is seen as a detriment rather than an aid in one's worship. The stress in these types of Evangelical outreach is a personal encounter that must be translated into an expression of public witness. Here, Scripture is of primary importance where cultural values must be reconciled with biblical understanding in order to have any merit. Thus, some aspects of the Korean culture can be tolerated, such as respect for one's elders when seen as one of the Ten Commandments and not as a requirement of Confucianism. The problem with this approach for Korean Americans is that it fails to appropriate a rightful place for one's culture, the historical and social context where revelation can only be truly integrated into one's being.

The "divorce" of Korean culture from religion for Korean American Protestants stems from their experiences on college campuses.[7] Evangelical influences during these formative academic years have left an indelible mark on the next generation of Korean American Protestants. Believing that faith should be void of culture and maintained solely on Christian principles, Korean American Protestants have gravitated toward an Evangelical model that appears free from cultural conditioning. From their perspective, some of the faith practices of their parents in immigrant churches have more affinity to Korean culture than to the Gospel message. However, the Evangelical model subscribed to by many of the younger generation Korean Americans is not conditioned free of culture. Even Evangelicals are conditioned by their situation in life. Influenced by the dominant Euro-American society and culture, Evangelicals appear void of cultural influences, especially since Euro-Americans are not considered one among many other cultures. However, Evangelicalism has been culturally conditioned as well. Euro-American

[7] Ibid., 5.

values are overlooked since the dominant culture is rarely questioned or regarded as just one of many ethnic cultures in our church and society. Rather, Evangelicalism is under similar cultural conditioning where the dominant Euro-American ethos has influenced the way this belief system is understood, expressed, and passed on.

Tensions between the next generations of Korean American Protestants and their parents' style of worshiping emphasizing the Korean culture has left many of the younger believers to distance themselves both culturally and religiously from their upbringing. Rather than continuing the religious practices of the immigrant generation, Korean American Protestants are creating a religious space that they believe is free of cultural ties and more authentic and faithful to the Word of God. The separation of Korean culture from one's religious practices is not a novelty since Protestants in Korea have also compartmentalized the two. Korean Protestants have infused some Confucian and shamanic thought on their belief systems. However, they have not been able to meld Korean cultural, social, and traditional practices into their worship.[8]

Whereas the lack of integration of Korean social and cultural practices with the worship style of Korean Protestants has been attributed to the brief history of Protestantism in Korea, the lack of integration of Korean American Protestants' practices with their parent group stems from a difference in religious ideology. In addition, where Protestants in Korea lack a cultural identity in their religiosity, immigrants maintain their cultural heritage through their religious experience. Thus, the immigrant Korean churches help maintain culture, language, and identity. As previously discussed, this use of religious space for maintaining one's cultural heritage does not sit well for the next generation of Korean American Protestants. The Korean ideals based on Confucianism are seen as "betrayals" since they are not scripturally founded. Therefore, the religious space newly created by Korean Americans tends either to avoid these cultural influences or to redefine them in light of the Scriptures. For example, filial piety and excellence in education are observed by Korean American Protestants not because of Confucian ideals but rather as a commandment of God where obedience and honor of one's parents is an imperative of Scripture.

[8] Ibid., 3.

CHAPTER 7

Pastoral Strategies

Balancing Generations: St. Thomas, Anaheim, California

St. Thomas Korean Catholic Center in Anaheim, California, is one of three ministries to the Korean American and immigrant population in the Diocese of Orange in Southern California. Although St. Thomas is not the oldest of the three centers, being an offshoot of the oldest neighboring ministry, it is today the largest in the diocese and considered one of the largest in the nation. Thus, the growth and ministerial presence of St. Thomas Korean Catholic Center is a hopeful sign for all Korean ministries. This hope comes, however, not solely from the number of parishioners or the size of buildings but rather from the process of transition this community has undergone from an exclusive ministry of the priests from Korea to the pastoral leadership of the local presbyterate. In turn, the presence of Korean American priests has also provided many opportunities for ministry to the next generation. Today, St. Thomas Korean Catholic Center is an effective outreach and ministry to the immigrant population as well as the next generation.

Fr. Alex Kim is the first Korean American priest ordained for the Diocese of Orange in 1991. After several parish assignments in the diocese, he was installed as the administrator of St. Thomas in 2001. Being installed as the spiritual leader, of then 4,200 parishioners, only opened the door for Fr. Kim into this community, thus providing an opportunity to implement his vision for Korean American ministry. Being the first has its privileged position, but this also means that the challenges are much more difficult to maneuver in uncharted waters. Some of these challenges arise from being a public spiritual figure of an ethnic community; however, certain challenges transcend occupation and social status for Korean Americans and are simply challenges the offspring of the immigrant group face as they attempt to navigate their lives blessed with the foundation of a Korean heritage expressed in the realities of the U.S.

Being a Korean American priest and not a priest from Korea meant that Fr. Kim would have to earn the trust and confidence of the initial immigrant group, his parents' peers, and the founders of the community in Anaheim, a trust and confidence that are usually granted automatically to missioner priests from Korea. The situation Fr. Kim faced is not unusual as the next generation, even as priests, encounter inevitable biases of their parents' generation. Whereas Korean missioners are almost naturally embraced as the spiritual leaders by the Korean-speaking immigrant group because of the Confucian ideals of a familial society, they seldom have any relationship with the next generation of English speakers. Korean American priests, on the other hand, have the opposite challenge as they are easily embraced by the English-speaking next generation not because of any Confucian structures but rather because of their ability to relate with life experiences through a common language. Through this connection, Korean American priests are able to minister effectively to the next generation; however, this connection with the next generation can also be a detriment for Korean American priests with the initial immigrant group.

The connection with the 1.5 and the second generation of Korean Americans comes from a simple fact—being children of the immigrant experience. While this connection is a strength in ministering to the next generation, in reality it is a substantial barrier in effectively communicating to and pastoring the Korean-speaking immigrant group. One of the immediate challenges of any Korean American priest leading an intergenerational community is the acceptance by the entire community, especially by the older parishioners who, in this case, are the peers of Fr. Kim's parents. Seen as the son of—or the child of—the parent group is a label often inescapable because of the perceptions of the older generation. This presents an immense challenge when Korean American priests are seen as juniors rather than on equal footing to their Korean counterparts. This uneven relationship effectively makes any Korean American priest limited in pastoring a generational congregation of Korean descent. However, out of every challenge comes a wealth of possibilities that are able to transcend the generational hurdles of such ethnic faith communities.

In addition to the generational barrier reinforced by filial conceptions of Confucian society—where the age of the person is also taken into account when the priestly figure is younger than most of the initial immigrants—Korean American priests must also overcome linguistic challenges on two levels. On the one hand, Korean American priests must be proficient in Korean as well as in English, since competency in both languages is a measuring rod of sorts in effective pastoral ministry. Obviously, a double standard exists here as Korean missioners are not expected to have such proficiency in both languages. The latter is expected to be fluent only in Korean since he is a missioner with the primary focus of his ministry to the Korean-speaking congregation. However, the former is expected to be fluent in both languages, especially when one's formative years of education are completed in this country. English is to be learned in society and Korean is to be maintained in the homes and through church programs like Korean Saturday school programs.

On the other hand, linguistic proficiency entails one's ability not only to speak the language but also to think in the mind-set of each ethnicity to effectively communicate the Gospel message in a particular cultural setting. The formation of Korean American priests in U.S. seminaries allows for pastoral sensitivities to differing ethnic groups. However, even with this attention to ministering in ethnic communities, immense challenges are present as theological categories differ with every changing context. Thus, the categories and means of communicating effectively here in this culture do not always translate and resonate with the mind-set of the immigrant communities. One of the main reasons why ethnic faith communities desire a pastoral leader similar to them is the comfort the familiar categories of communication afford each group.

The linguistic challenges alone are major hurdles in ministering to Korean immigrants and the next generation. The challenges within are both cultural and generational for these ethnic ministries in the U.S. Thus, the way the Gospel message is conveyed to each generation must also be cultivated along with ethnic sensitivity. Terminology, concepts, and imagery that work in one generation do not always translate to the next. This has always been the challenge of the Gospel, a challenge of evangelization to present the realities of Jesus Christ, the fullness of revelation, as found in Scripture and Tradition, into a relatable experience of today.

Recently, parochial vicars are becoming more noticeable in large Korean Catholic communities across the U.S., especially in light of the great numbers of vocations to the priesthood in Korea. While such luxuries of having two priests in one community address some of the pastoral concerns of these large ethnic communities, they still illustrate the lack of ministerial attention to the next generation as well as the inability of such missioners to embrace the differing mind-set. Once again, the linguistic challenges of these ethnic communities limit pastoral effectiveness. Korean missioners, even younger parochial vicars, are not able to overcome these pastoral limitations. Younger priests from Korea still cater to the immigrant group by ministering to the newly arrived young people, especially as foreign students, since this is within their comfort zone both culturally, generationally, and linguistically. In short, they do not end up ministering in English. Obviously, this model of evangelization fails to resonate with the next generation of English-speaking Korean American Catholics. The U.S. experience with Korean missioners has been an invaluable one. Without their priestly presence, the ethnic faith communities would have never matured to the levels of today. However, the ongoing missioners from Korea are also signifying a tension with the U.S. experience of these ethnic communities as the initial immigrant groups are still receiving the majority of pastoral care, while the older immigrant groups and especially their offspring find themselves on the fringes of some of these communities in the U.S. In particular, the smaller, more rural area communities experience this tension in much more drastic ways than the bigger, more metropolitan churches where the numbers of parishioners deflect the cultural and generational issues.

Given these challenges of ministering to the Korean-speaking immigrant group and English-speaking next generation, Fr. Kim's achievements with both groups at St. Thomas Korean Catholic Center is quite a historic achievement. Fr. Kim not only overcame the barriers as a Korean American priest to effectively minister to the immigrant generation but has done so to the level of shattering the biases held between both groups. As painful as the initial prejudice of the immigrant generation was for this pastor, his commitment to a ministerial vision for this community allowed for such radical transformation and growth.

In fairness to others laboring in similar pastoral situations, Fr. Kim is not without certain advantages that allowed St. Thomas to become a leading spiritual center in Southern California and an ecclesial model for ethnic ministries. At least four advantages come to mind that may make the St. Thomas experience unique and not replicable in other parts of the U.S. For one thing, being in Orange County and starting a new ministry with cultural and generational sensitivity when it was much needed is a huge advantage because of the population size of those of Korean descent. Neighboring Korean and Korean American Protestant Churches in the area reflect the fertile ground in the northern regions of Orange County. Next, even with other Korean ministries previously existing in Orange County, the pastoral successes of many of these ministries were limited and never fully matured for the next generation. In addition, the immigrant generation and especially the next generation of Korean Americans needed enough time to mature themselves for such ecclesial

developments. Finally, Fr. Kim's own pastoral experience needed time
to germinate and flourish before his priestly presence could lead such
an expression of the Korean American Catholic faith. Thus, the perfect
storm—one involving the maturation of the Korean American and immigrant population as well as the development of priestly leadership to
converge together in Anaheim, California—allowed St. Thomas Catholic
Center to be what it is today.

The question of whether this experience of church is replicable elsewhere can be heavily debated. Regardless, St. Thomas Korean Catholic
Center is a hopeful model for others when enough time and resources
come together, in terms of both priestly presence and the laity. Patience
and vision are two qualities we are reminded of from this ethnic ecclesial
experience in Southern California. As an offshoot of the original community where Koreans gathered, St. Thomas underwent many growth
stages like many other ethnic faith communities. Being in a small center
for their weekday activities while borrowing a local high school audito-
rium for their Sunday gatherings, St. Thomas began like so many other
Korean immigrant faith gatherings. From these small beginnings, St.
Thomas has become an active presence for the faith life of Korean Americans as well as for continuing immigrants. There are many lessons to be
learned in this local experience of church; however, two in particular are
necessary for every community, regardless of culture and generations.
First, with any faith community, pastoral vision is an absolute necessity.
One cannot simply be church without this element that arises from the
synthesis of pastoral leadership and the faith of the laity. Second, patience
is a must, since the maturation process of any community requires time,
and sometimes in the case of ethnic ministries, it requires generations.
With patience and a vision of where the faith life is headed, church in
any cultural and generational context becomes pertinent to the lives of
the faithful, especially the lives of the immigrant people and the next
generation.

To be church means that our faith must transcend cultures and generations. If not, church fails to exist as her mission of internal and external
evangelization and renewal becomes absent. All ethnic faith communities
are a reminder that a sign of health is the renewal on these two levels.
For this particular faith community, their expression of the faith even in
a particular cultural setting has transcended the people of Korean descent
as a Tongan community now resides with them. Rather than going to a
local parish, the Tongan community in Orange County has made their
home within the Korean center. Participating in the English-speaking

liturgy, the Tongan people are able to preserve their cultural identity while becoming one at the table of the Lord with others. This Tongan presence presents many questions to the local diocesan and parish structures. For one, why would another ethnic faith group feel more at home in another ethnic community rather than in the larger parish community?

Making one feel at home is another quality of the pastoral leadership of Fr. Kim as well as the entire faith community of St. Thomas. Today, there are 5,600 parishioners with ten vocations to the priesthood and religious life (nine men and one woman). Although there is not a consensus of how multicultural, multiethnic, and now multigenerational liturgies should be conducted, St. Thomas accommodates the various dimensions of the Korean American people by offering a comfort zone for worship. Rather than celebrating liturgies together, Masses are celebrated in either Korean or English, and parishioners are encouraged to attend the liturgies that are most comfortable. The strength of this pastoral approach is that parishioners will understand the prayers because of linguistic familiarity. The drawback of such an approach is that intergenerational unity is hard to come by as families will continue to attend separate Masses. However, the pastoral approach embraced by Fr. Kim and the faithful of St. Thomas allows everyone, including Tongans, to feel at home with the liturgical celebrations in the language of most accessibility. Fortunately, St. Thomas is able to provide both Korean and English Masses on Sundays by a Korean priest. Often, this is not the case since the English Masses at most Korean centers are not celebrated by a familiar Korean face but by a priest of a differing ethnicity. Thus, the English Mass at St. Thomas is the second most attended liturgy out of the four Sunday gatherings.

Along with the comforts of one's language, space is a must for ministries to thrive for these ethnic faith communities. While most parishes focus on Mass attendance, lending to a large sanctuary space for a one hour gathering, Catholics of Korean descent need much more gathering room for longer periods of time. Since church is not a one-hour reality, given the cultural, social, and religious components of a Sunday gathering, Korean immigrants and the next generation engage in their cultural faith by sharing a meal together at the eucharistic table as well as in the dining hall afterward. From these two types of nourishment, the faithful continue their Sunday spiritual journey by continuing to meet in smaller prayer groups, catechetical studies, and fellowship.

The experience of St. Thomas Korean Catholic Center is due to several elements coming together. From the social arena to the spiritual, Korean American Catholics needed to come into their own to dictate such a ministry. In addition, a spiritual leader such as Fr. Alex Kim who overcame the biases of the initial immigrant group to effectively pastor not only the Korean-speaking congregation but, equally important, the English-speaking next generation was essential. The perfect storm bringing together personnel, people, and the expanded space in Anaheim allowed this particular Korean American ministry to truly become a model of hope for the local church as well as the universal.

Shared Parish: St. Robert Bellarmine, Bayside, New York

In many ways, St. Robert Bellarmine Catholic Church in Bayside, New York, in the Diocese of Brooklyn, is much like many other older Catholic communities in the U.S. that are undergoing demographic transitions. Located on Queens in New York City, St. Robert Bellarmine church, school, rectory, convent, and gym encompass an entire city block. The church is located a few blocks from Northern Boulevard, which has become the hub for Korean American businesses. The original Italian and Irish immigrants who once heavily populated the parish boundaries have now gotten older. Their children have moved away and the Catholic faith, which often helped minority groups preserve their identity and culture, is no longer as valued by succeeding generations.

One important consequence of the changing racial and ethnic demographics is the significant decline of Euro-American English-speaking Mass goers on Sundays. The pastor of St. Robert Bellarmine, Msgr. Martin Geraghty, calls this change the "Asianification" of Bayside, since housing and businesses are becoming predominantly occupied by Asian Americans. Moving into the parish boundaries today are Korean and Chinese Americans, who value the high academic achievements of the local public school district. In many ways, St. Robert Bellarmine in Bayside is much like other Catholic communities facing new challenges with shifting parish demographics. However, what makes St. Robert Bellarmine particularly noteworthy is the diocesan and parish outreach to the Korean American community in the midst of changing demographics.

In response to the changing signs of the times, Bishop Nicholas DiMarzio, Auxiliary Bishop Frank J. Caggiano, and Msgr. Geraghty have taken a novel strategic approach. Rather than resisting the changing demographics, Msgr. Geraghty, along with other church leaders of the diocese, has embraced the "Asianification" of this parish. By doing so, Msgr. Geraghty has become a "grandfatherly" figure for the growing Catholic population of Korean descent. Like his predecessors, Msgr. Geraghty has meticulously kept weekly Sunday attendance data that show the shifting demographics of his parish in order to respond appropriately to the needs of his parishioners. At present, approximately 35 to 40 percent of Sunday's attendance consists of Korean Americans. However, the Korean immigrant community has only one Sunday Mass while there are four English Masses for the majority of the parishioners. The tipping point for St. Robert Bellarmine transitioning from a primarily English-speaking community to a Korean community is somewhere on the horizon. Instead of resisting this transition as pastors sometimes do, Msgr. Geraghty and the Brooklyn diocese have taken proactive measures not only to welcome the Korean-speaking congregation to St. Robert Bellarmine but also to create a novel outreach to the overall Asian community residing within the parish boundaries, regardless of religious affiliation.

From humble beginnings, St. Robert Bellarmine began with a congregation of about four hundred members with the celebration of the first Mass on January 22, 1939. The name for the parish was chosen in honor of the saint's recent canonization in 1930. Parish construction was completed and dedicated on May 18, 1941, on what was previously the site of Bayside Hill's golf course. The need for a larger church was evident by the 1960s when twelve thousand people became the normal Sunday population as twelve Masses, which were celebrated with the assistance of visiting clergy. Given such vitality and growth, a new St. Robert Bellarmine church was constructed in 1969.

Originating in a neighboring church, St. Paul Ha Sang in Flushing, New York, and then branching off to St. Robert Bellarmine, the Korean American community was established on February 9, 1997. The first Korean-speaking priest of the newly formed community, Msgr. Thomas Kyung Hwan Kim, was appointed at the end of April 1999. St. Robert Bellarmine has been fortunate in having several Korean-speaking priests, including a Korean American priest, Fr. Andrew Kim, a priest ordained in the Diocese of Brooklyn, who served this community for over seven years. Along with the Korean-speaking clergy, the Sisters of Korean Martyrs continue to serve the parish needs.

At present, the total number of parishioners is a fraction of those in the 1950s and 1960s. Currently, the four English Sunday Masses attract roughly one thousand to twelve hundred parishioners—fewer than three hundred per Mass—while the one Korean Mass is attended by 465 to 500 parishioners on any given Sunday. In addition to these changing numbers, another interesting dynamic exists between the clergy at St. Robert Bellarmine. The Irish American pastor, Msgr. Martin Geraghty, was born in Brooklyn in 1940. As many in his generation, he began studies for the priesthood at an early age and was ordained in Rome in 1964. After teaching theology for eighteen years in an undergraduate seminary program at Cathedral College and then serving as pastor of English-speaking communities another eighteen years, Msgr. Geraghty became pastor of St. Robert Bellarmine in 2006.

Msgr. Geraghty has been gracious with the Korean-speaking community and is revered as a "grandfatherly" figure possessing much wisdom. A positive exchange between the English-speaking pastor and the Korean community exists, which is not always the case in shared parish models. His parochial vicars serving the Korean-speaking community have come from the local diocese or from the Korean Diocese of Daejeon (Taejon). Having a parochial vicar from another diocese, let alone another country, is an interesting dynamic, one that seems to peacefully coexist. In contrast, when a Korean missioner is subordinate to an English-speaking pastor, and when the Korean community feels like they only "rent" space from the dominant congregation, they frequently tend to move out to build their own church. Building their own church is characteristic of the initial immigrant generation taking ownership in their new host country within familiar confines.

In 2008, a museum exhibit, sponsored by the City of New York, explored "the social and political history of the diverse group of people who established the formidable Catholic presence in New York." The historical beginnings of the parochial school system in the United States were portrayed as a part of this exploration as the exhibit examined how a "community of immigrants" preserved its Catholic identity. Although Catholic schools continue in New York to the present day, the museum curators ended the exhibit with 1946, the end of World War II, as urban Catholics began relocating to the suburbs. Thus, the museum exhibit chose the Second World War as the close of the Catholic school era because of the demographic shift in the population of the United States. Catholic schools addressed many issues revolving around the inner-city and immigrant communities in their inception. After the Second World War, the suburbanization of the population created a new environment into which Catholic schools naturally moved with the parishioners.

According to this portrayal, the migration of parochial schools into the suburbs affected the philosophy, goals, and outlook of Catholic education. Thus, the end of an era of urban Catholic schools marks the beginning of a new way of being a parochial school in a suburban environment. The church, not fully aware of this transition, continued to model its educational outreach in a similar fashion to the past that worked in industrial, urban, and immigrant neighborhoods. Today, many of the issues affecting Catholic schools can be traced to this period of transition where the church did not fully adapt to the changing demographics, a movement from urban neighborhoods into the suburbs. Aware of another shift in demographics on the horizon, St. Robert Bellarmine and the Diocese of Brooklyn are making preparations in order to address the needs of the people living in their parish boundaries.

Perhaps St. Robert Bellarmine will never regain the numbers of the past. However, the pastoral vision given the shifting demographics has sparked new life in the parish. Still in a very embryonic stage, the diocese and Msgr. Geraghty are evangelizing the Asian American communities of Bayside, in particular Korean Americans, by targeting what most concerns the changing demographic population. Because most of those moving into the parish boundaries are concerned about the educational achievements of the local public schools, the parish school at St. Robert Bellarmine is re-creating itself not only as a model of academic excellence but also as a model of Korean American academic excellence providing what parents of Asian American students most desire.

The Brooklyn diocese has decided to revamp its parish structures through consolidation and closures. In terms of parish schools, the diocese has decided to take the approach of charter schools by establishing new lay leadership boards to oversee the day-to-day operations rather than placing these responsibilities on the pastors. Accordingly, a parochial school would become a Catholic academy run by a lay leadership board. The pastor would be responsible for the Catholic identity of the academy, but every other aspect would be the responsibility of the lay leadership board.

Established as a Catholic academy in September 2011, St. Robert Bellarmine instituted a new academic program to reach its goal of academic excellence. However, just a good academic outlook is not enough to attract Korean Americans or any other Asian Americans, since the public school system can do an equal if not better job at this in this particular school district. Thus, another way of targeting Korean Americans to consider St. Robert Bellarmine as an educational alternative over well-established, overachieving public schools is to offer a complete academic package.

Korean American students often attend afterschool programs known as *hagwons*, which offer educational assistance in subjects in which a student may be deficient and/or test preparation courses (e.g., SAT).

These *hagwons* cost parents thousands of dollars annually and without them parents often feel they are not providing their children with all the necessary tools to get ahead in life. Thus, St. Robert Bellarmine's evangelical outreach includes a *hagwon* program in their academic outreach. Instead of sending students elsewhere after school for further educational assistance, St. Robert Bellarmine is offering similar programs in their own facility. In addition to the bonus afterschool *hagwon* program, St. Robert Bellarmine hopes to attract students through its appeal as a Catholic institution emphasizing faith and morality in the upbringing of any child.

With this novel evangelical approach in Catholic education through targeting a certain demographic population, St. Robert Bellarmine and the Diocese of Brooklyn are not only trying to keep alive the parish school but, more importantly, adapting parish resources to welcome the evolving population of Bayside, New York. Noteworthy in this endeavor is that the Korean American community is highlighted in a pastoral plan. Often, Korean Americans are not given many directives or opportunities from the hierarchy of a diocese. Small ethnic groups are often left alone or overlooked in pastoral planning, especially if the pastors of those communities are foreigners with limited English communication skills. What is unique in this situation is that the Korean American community has become a priority for the "survival" of the parish community. With this priority come directives, resources, and pastoral planning already occurring on the diocesan level as well as the parish level.

On June 30, 2010, Bishop Caggiano met with the pastoral councils and other lay leaders of all the Korean American Catholic communities within the Diocese of Brooklyn in a town hall type of format, first to propose the evangelical outreach to Korean Americans and second to begin the dialogue for such a commitment from both sides. The initial reaction was typical as Korean Americans present at the meeting raised sustainability concerns, such as population numbers and additional financial burdens because of this outreach. However, this shortsightedness does not reveal the immense value not only for Korean American Catholics in Bayside, New York, or even the diocese but the vision this pastoral planning could create for the rest of the country in terms of outreach to Korean American communities throughout the U.S.

The benefits outweigh the immediate burdens on Korean Americans. First, a Korean American Catholic community becoming a focus of a diocesan pastoral plan is a huge step in gaining recognition and resources for any future planning. Not often do Korean American communities receive the attention from the hierarchical leadership regarding their existence as an ethnic community. Second, the relevance of such a model of evangelization is beneficial not only to the rest of the diocese but for other dioceses with similar changing demographics. If the Catholic academy and its pursuit of excellence by providing an all-inclusive package including an afterschool *hagwon* program is effective, then it becomes an attractive model for others in various parts of the country. Third, the increased interest in St. Robert Bellarmine by such an evangelization and outreach program should also impact Sunday attendance numbers. With an increase in Mass attendance, St. Robert Bellarmine would naturally evolve into a Korean American parish, the first of its kind in many ways, that would still be multicultural; however, the once-minority group would now become the majority.

There are many criticisms raised when targeting a specific ethnic group in its evangelical outreach. However, this new approach and the ramifications it has for all Korean American ministries needs to be fostered if any other future Korean American pastoral plans are to develop. Ethnic groups such as Korean Americans have been simply called to model the dominant Euro-American English-speaking communities for too long. This example provides an opportunity to be creative as a church to reach out not only to the existing community but, more importantly, to succeeding generations. Success is not whether the Catholic academy outreach to Korean Americans works. Success is the ability to accommodate and welcome others by reaching out to their needs regardless of their numbers.

Regional Outreach:
CUNAE, Northeast U.S. Young Adult Charismatic Ministry

With limited numbers and resources facing young adults at Korean American centers in any diocese throughout the U.S., a regional model of pastoral outreach has often been employed. Some outreach programs aimed at Korean American young adults are intercultural, and others are bilingual; some are limited to a diocesan geographic area, and others span multiple dioceses; some are led by lay leadership, and others have diocesan or religious clergy as their spiritual guides; some work in cooperation with the local parishes, and others have tensions over such scarce resources; some are limited to college-age students on their campuses, and others include young adults from eighteen years old into their forties. In short, the all-around scarcities within this demographic group along with the pastoral vision of certain clergy members are what define and drive young adult ministry. It is safe to say that many attempts at gathering young adults through both English- and Korean-speaking ministries have come and gone. It is also safe to say that many more attempts will be made locally and regionally to unite young adults, mainly because of the lack of place within the immigrant model of Korean ministry.

One regional outreach model that has been touching the lives of many Korean American young adults on the Eastern seaboard is CUNAE currently based out of the Archdiocese of Newark, New Jersey. Originally created in cooperation with the priests of the Brooklyn diocese to serve the needs of young adults in the New York and New Jersey area through the charismatic renewal, today it is largely guided by Korean American priests of the local area serving Korean American young adults as far north as Boston, south as Atlanta, and east as Philadelphia. CUNAE is a Latin phrase referring to the nest of young birds. The ministry of CUNAE is the symbolic nest where young adults come to find their place and grow in their faith. Through their weekly prayer meetings, seasonal retreats, and annual conference, CUNAE has encouraged young adults to experience the Lord through a personal encounter with the Holy Spirit and to grow in the gifts that benefit the CUNAE community as well as their own parishes.

Like most charismatic movements, members are invited to the group through their retreats, focusing on their personal encounter with the Holy Spirit, receiving spiritual gifts, and then living them out within the CUNAE community as well as their own local parishes. After the retreat experience with the CUNAE community, participants may choose to become active members by participating in regular prayer groups. In addition to dedicated volunteers, a priest is assigned as the spiritual guide. Members of CUNAE dedicate much time and energy as many commute long distances and costly toll bridges to continue their spiritual growth within this community on a weekly basis. On weekends, many are also active members in their local parishes, fulfilling vital ministries in their local churches. A common characteristic of many members of CUNAE is that they are stretched thin between work, church, and CUNAE.

This charismatic outreach model originated approximately twenty years ago for this region. The adult participants of the Korean charismatic movement, known as CRSC-NE, were concerned about the younger generation and wanted to share their faith experience with them. Initially inviting young adults into their own community and way of prayer, CRSC-NE members eventually encouraged those in attendance to branch off and begin a similar ministry strictly for young adults in the northeastern part of the U.S. The first two pioneering young adult leaders were not only influential in the beginning stages of CUNAE but continue their spiritual leadership today as a priest and religious sister. Other vocations to the priesthood or to the service to the church have developed from this young adult community. There are many places where young adults can go for a charismatic experience or any other liturgical prayer. However, there are few places where Korean American young adults are able to create their own space, their own community. CUNAE provides a charismatic experience, but also, more importantly, an ecclesial community to grow in their faith. Thus, this growth is twofold. On the one hand, a nurturing place (a nest) is provided. On the other hand, a sense of mission, especially singling out to whom we should minister, is instilled through this gathering. This twofold experience propels many to continue to serve in the church on behalf of other Korean Americans.

With twenty years of ministerial experience, CUNAE members look to embed themselves permanently in the Korean American ecclesial landscape in the Northeast. Recently, a constitution was drafted, a first for many regional ministries, to ensure that the mission, work, planning, and service of CUNAE will continue regardless of the changing of lay and priestly leadership. As the original pioneers and other members of this young adult movement have moved on within the twenty years, the constitution incorporates a faithfulness to those who laid the foundation for this ministry while at the same time widening the vision to do other creative ministry on behalf of Korean American young adults.

The one interesting thing in reading through their constitution is that CUNAE refers to themselves and their ministries as Korean young adults. When asked about this and not the term "Korean American," one of the editors of the constitution mentioned that it never crossed their minds. The irony in all this is that some of the current core leaders of CUNAE were born in the U.S. Both Korean and English are used in ministering to young adults, and many would hardly associate with only one culture or the other. However, these young adults are truly Korean Americans, being able to navigate both their secular and religious worlds.

The inability to distinguish between themselves as Koreans or Korean Americans can be attributed to several factors, the first being their origination from a Korean-only parent group, where their identity as a branch of and still dependent on the parent group funding. CUNAE members still view themselves as part of the whole while ministering to a specific demographic group. Therefore, "Korean young adult ministry" to CUNAE rather than "Korean American young adult ministry" retains continuity and support. Another factor for not distinguishing between the two is that the young adult generation has not reached a common consciousness. Without such a consciousness, this distinction never enters into a person's mind. Korean and Korean American terminology are interchangeable in this outreach. Finally, the use of "Korean" rather than "Korean Americans" reflects a lack of self-identity and ownership in some instances.

A recent study on young adults in the U.S. generically characterizes this demographic regardless of ethnicity as being (1) non-committal so they can always leave their options open for a better opportunity, (2) never having enough financial resources, and (3) with an uncertain purpose where they sometimes visualize the "good life" but cannot concretize it in their own lives.[9] This status for many young adults, in particular Korean Americans, translates into a lack of ownership for many. CUNAE and other outreach ministries are trying to increase the ownership of church and society for young adults by the commitment and dedication necessary for its own growth and mission. Still, young adults are in flux as they navigate their work, family, and church. Once young adults are able to claim as their own the religious space, particular ministry, and place in society, their identities as Korean Americans will become more concretized. Once they take ownership and create their spiritual and career paths, generations of Korean descent will be able to truly appreciate their heritage and their distinction as different yet similar to the parent group. CUNAE is an opportunity for such a consciousness and are providing the foundation for the realization of a specific group.

[9] Christian Smith, *Souls in Transitions: The Religious and Spiritual Lives of Emerging Adults* (Oxford: Oxford University Press, 2009).

CHAPTER 8

Lessons from Departure, Displacement, and Resettlement

Chuseok (추석)

Chuseok is one of the most important annual celebrations for Koreans. Stemming from an agricultural society and in thanksgiving for another prosperous harvest, *chuseok* is celebrated as both a communal and a filial occasion on the fifteenth day of the eighth month of the lunar calendar. Similar to the U.S. Thanksgiving tradition, this holiday serves multiple social, cultural, and religious purposes. The origins of this ceremony are unknown, but legend has it that the thanksgiving festivities of *chuseok* are attributed to the lunar activities emphasizing the uniqueness of the full moon since the sun is constant in size throughout the year. Celebrated today as a national holiday, *chuseok* allows Koreans and Korean Americans to maintain their social, cultural, and religious heritage.

As a social celebration, *chuseok* is a time to gather with extended family and to continue the filial piety traditions by recognizing family members both living and deceased. Traditionally, people return to their hometowns, symbolically returning to their roots. In preparation for the family gathering, traditional food and gifts are prepared in order to give thanks for the year's abundant harvest, especially important back when Korea was mostly an agrarian society. In addition to the gathering and meal in honor of one's ancestors, there are annual visits to family gravesites. During these graveside visits, one pays respect to the deceased family members. Today, the congestion of people leaving a metropolitan city such as Seoul all at once makes life very difficult. Thus, a reverse visit is also occurring where those outside of Seoul gather as one family within the confines of the city even though Seoul is not the family's hometown. This is an important reality for Korean Americans, since the departure from Korea as immigrants meant that *chuseok* could never be celebrated in the same manner. For immigrants such as Korean Catholics, *chuseok* is still an important occasion; however, the inability to fulfill one's filial obligations places this social and cultural celebration in an awkward context due to geography and the inability of families to always gather during this occasion. Today, the tradition of gathering during *chuseok*, recognizing one's ancestors, and giving thanks continues as a cultural reminder within a religious context—similar to the traditional manner, yet unique due to the immigration experience.

As a cultural celebration, *chuseok* affords the Korean people an occasion to maintain their cultural dress, food, dance, and play. Along with the family gatherings, festivities during this celebration allow Koreans to celebrate their cultural uniqueness. *Chuseok* festivities include a traditional meal known as *chare* (차례), where the main table is arranged in a way to honor deceased family members. For example, the meal is prepared on a table facing north with the best portions nearest the deceased or away from those present. In particular, the best portions of the meal are set to the right of the deceased members. There are also food restrictions for this ceremonial meal. For example, kimchee—one of the staple foods for all Koreans—is to be avoided during the meal preparation for the *chuseok* table.

Translation and adaptations of these cultural events for immigrants and subsequent generations are necessary since geographical distance and resource limitations make the cultural rituals difficult to maintain in new locales. The translation of these cultural significances allows immigrants and their descendants to maintain a connection to their heritage while allowing the transformation of the same heritage as it takes root in a new soil. These familiar yet unique expressions of the cultural significances of Korea should not be seen as inferior manifestations but rather a continuation of the cultural expressions of Korean descendants. Just as new forms appear in Seoul where the metropolitan lifestyle makes it difficult to gather outside the city and thus a reverse family visit is occurring, the manner in which Korean Americans gather should be encouraged and recognized as important and valid celebrations of the family ceremony as well.

Traditionally, *chuseok* contains much religious significance to the ritual as well. The honoring of ancestors is found in most cultural and religious influences of Korea. Culturally, Confucian teaching emphasizes filial piety as well as respect for one's elders. Thus, the ritual actions of *chuseok* honoring the deceased while gathering together as a family in the presence of one's elders continue the Confucian notion of filial piety and thought. Religiously, the notion of the spirit world in shamanism on Korean society plays an important part of *chuseok*'s understanding of honoring the deceased family members. By acknowledging the spirits of deceased members in this meal ritual, shamanic undertones become apparent through its connection to the spirit world. Modern religious overtones have also influenced the practices of Korean American Catholics in regards to *chuseok*. Unable to bridge the gap between geographic locations, where returning to one's hometown and to family members is nearly impossible, some Korean immigrants have focused *chuseok's* importance on the communal religious worship. By emphasizing religious worship through liturgical celebrations, Catholics of Korean descent are able to maintain their *chuseok* obligations by having a traditional meal at home as well as partaking in the eucharistic meal at church.

The gathering for the family meal along with the communal celebration continues modern-day *chuseok* traditions. The household ritual of the *chuseok* ceremony highlights the religious ritual at the Lord's table. By partaking in a meal with family members gathered together as best they can, centered in the home of loved ones, *chuseok* is celebrated as it would be back in Korea where family members are remembered and honored. This time, the remembering is not only for those who have departed from this life but also for those who could not gather because of great distances as well as those who have undergone departure, displacement, and resettlement. As the family meal is shared, it becomes apparent that not all transitions and translations of the traditional *chuseok* can be realized. One of the difficulties in observing the time-honored filial traditions is the visitation to the family's gravesite. Some have outsourced the responsibilities of maintaining the gravesite while others, such as my own family, have transported the remains of the deceased relatives for burial in family plots in the U.S. During the 1980s, my grandparents' remains were brought over from their Korean countryside graves so that proper visitation and respect could be paid to them here in the States. Even with this accommodation, the reality of our dispersed lives still makes this aspect of *chuseok* difficult to observe.

Catholicism is transforming our modern understanding of the *chuseok* celebration as obligations are maintained and fulfilled through the practices of the Catholic faith. By transforming Korean traditional practices with the Catholic notions of the communion of saints, prayers for the departed, and the sharing in the eucharistic meal, the immigrant communities are able to preserve and fulfill their ritual obligations away from Korean soil. The communion of saints, where those who have gone before the faithful present are still able to assist those in the world, continues the filial respect found in Korean culture. Through the Catholic understanding of church on earth and the church in heaven, the departed as well as the living are able to intercede for one another. The living assists the departed in the purification process on the way to their eternal reward; in particular, by offering the Mass for the dead. The prayers from those who have gone before us in faith, especially those who lived a life worthy of recognition by the church, are also requested on behalf of those in this world seeking to walk a similar road of honor and holiness.

The eucharistic meal is what truly completes the *chuseok* ceremony for Catholics of Korean descent. Similar to the family meal, the communal gathering at church re-creates, replaces, and reinvents some of the missing cultural aspects. Symbolic and religious connections between the eucharistic sharing and *chuseok* become evident under closer examination. Symbolically, the Eucharist allows everyone to partake in the one meal that truly nourishes regardless of geographic location. The gathering at the table of the Lord represents the family gathering at the *chuseok* table in one's hometown. By focusing on the spiritual house, Catholics are able to re-create, replace, and reimage what it means to gather as one family through the union that is found in communion.

Religiously, the eucharistic sharing expresses the spiritual components of the *chuseok* ceremony. As the sacrament *par excellence*, the Eucharist signifies that through the actions of Jesus' life, death, and resurrection, we are able to enter into union with God the Father while at the same time being in communion with one another as the body of our Lord. The unity of the ecclesial family brought about by our sharing at the table of the Lord allows Catholics of Korean descent to enter into another reality, one that is centered on the heavenly banquet where all of God's children are called to gather. Thus, the Liturgy of the Eucharist is the sacrificial meal that remembers and honors the past, allows us to be fully present, and directs us to our future home.

In the Korean-language liturgy, Eucharistic Prayer II is often used for its brevity and familiarity. The schema from this eucharistic prayer provides an illustration of how some religious elements of *chuseok* parallel the Catholic liturgy. During the consecration, the bread and wine become the Body and Blood of Christ through the words and actions of the eucharistic prayer of thanksgiving, *epiclesis*, institution narrative, *anamnesis*, and intercession. Naturally, *chuseok* as a way of giving thanks for a bountiful harvest connects easily with the Greek notion of thanksgiving found in our liturgical movements.

Eucharistic Prayer II begins with a prayer of thanksgiving recognizing God the Father as the fount and being of holiness. Following the words and act of thanksgiving, *epiclesis* calls down the Holy Spirit through the prayers and outstretched hands of the presider over the gifts of bread and wine. Next, the institution narrative recalls the words and actions of Jesus through the breaking of the bread and the sharing of the cup. *Anamnesis* is another way of remembering "as we celebrate the memorial of his Death and Resurrection."[1] Once again, the sacrifice and offering of Jesus is recalled through the bread of life and the chalice of salvation.

"Humbly we pray that, partaking of the Body and Blood of Christ, we may be gathered into one by the Holy Spirit" is also part of the *epiclesis* that comes after the institution. Just like the prior words and gesture of calling down the Holy Spirit upon the gifts on the altar, the words of *epiclesis* at this junction make the presence of Christ's body real as those who come to the table are made one. The eucharistic prayer then concludes with intercessions on behalf of the church, beginning with the Holy Pontiff, the local bishop, and all the clergy. The church's intercession may or may not specifically include a certain deceased member before continuing the prayers in general for all those who have "fallen asleep" and "died in your mercy." The intercession concludes with one final request on our own behalf: "Have mercy on us all, we pray, that with the Blessed Virgin Mary, Mother of God, with the blessed Apostles, and all the Saints who have pleased you throughout the ages, we may merit to be coheirs to eternal life, and may praise and glorify you through your Son, Jesus Christ."

The *chuseok* table is reminiscent of the table of the Lord. The sacrifice at the altar of the spotless lamb becomes the idealized table of communion of *chuseok*. In both rituals, giving thanks is the primary reason why families and the faithful gather together. While there is no equivalent of *epiclesis* where Catholics call upon the Holy Spirit for the transubstantiation of the gifts of bread and wine into the Body and Blood of Jesus Christ, the Korean *chuseok* ritual does recognize the need for assistance beyond one's own ability. Instead of attributing successes on the efforts of one's hard work, the *chuseok* ritual attributes these luxuries as the contributions of both the living and the dead in one's family.

The institution narrative in the Catholic liturgy represents the words and actions of Christ at the Last Supper. Although there are no structured narratives to follow in the *chuseok* ritual, the fellowship between family members both living and deceased constitutes a family narrative where the stories of the past become realized through the events of the present.

---

[1] All references to Eucharistic Prayer II are taken from the third English translation of the Roman Missal.

Through the ongoing narrative of one's family, a similar type of *anamnesis* occurs, since filial piety requires a manner of remembering one's elder. Thus, the gathering on this occasion allows for the family to continually intercede on one's behalf. The thanksgiving nature of *chuseok* for both the living and deceased indicates the interconnectedness of our lives where constant intercession is made on one another's behalf. Thus, the liturgical nature of prayer in the Catholic faith allows people of Korean descent to observe and maintain the *chuseok* experience by re-creating, replacing, and reimaging meaningful practices into the context of people's lives.

Without oversimplifying the connection between the table fellow-ships of the Eucharist and *chuseok*, I have structurally outlined the two rituals' parallelism to one another. However, I also realize the dangers of reducing elements to their lowest common denominators. Although more studies between the relationship of Eucharist and *chuseok* must be undertaken for an appropriate analysis of the two, there is no denying that *chuseok* has been influenced by Judeo-Christianity, especially here in the U.S. It is also difficult to determine whether the challenges of modern-day living, such as geographic distances between family members, is the impetus for a religious outlook of *chuseok* or whether the natural connec-tion between one's faith practices was realized in the Korean tradition of family preservation. The lives affected by immigration suggest that reasons and needs were mutual factors.

Bishop James Vincent Pardy, M.M.

The departure, displacement, and resettlement of Bishop James Pardy, not once, but twice, in his lifetime provide an invaluable lesson that all Koreans and Korean Americans must experience while carrying their cultural crosses of their past in a non-burdensome way. The Maryknoll missioner, Bishop Pardy, spent most of his priestly vocation in the Korean peninsula, serving his last eleven years there as the bishop of Cheongju (Ch'ongju). From 1958 to 1969, Bishop Pardy worked tirelessly in laying the foundation for today's rapidly growing church in Korea by fostering native vocations, strategic parish planning, and his love for the Korean people. His passion and dedication is the reason why the return of his remains to Korean soil over three decades later was a bittersweet occasion. Once Bishop Pardy retired and returned to the U.S., the people he once shepherded in his former diocese went on with their lives and failed to remember an intricate figure in their social and ecclesial history. Thus, upon his return to Korea in a small urn, Bishop Gabriel Chang greeted his former predecessor with gratitude, sadness, and humility. His words during the homily on November 30, 2011, captured the gamut of emotions during the transfer of the remains of Bishop Pardy.

> We have forgotten you completely, Bishop, and have gone on with our lives. We have forgotten your generosity and blessings and have gone on with our lives. No one went to see the forgotten bishop after his retirement; no one phoned you, nor did we send you a Christmas card. No one was there to watch at your death bed. For twenty-eight years after your death, no one visited your grave, and this is no exaggeration. They say that the greatest pain and sadness for parents is to be cast out by their children. They say that the greatest pain and sadness for parents, the greatest anger and despair that they can feel, is to be forgotten by the children they raised with love, the offspring they put their hope in, to live totally estranged. At this time let us all bend our knees and beg together that the bishop who gave us blessings like water during his long life will forgive us for our lack of filial piety.[2]

Bishop Pardy's journey to Korea as a missioner and his return to the U.S. represent a twofold transition from one community to another, exemplifying some stages of the immigration process between the two countries. With rupture from the homeland, obligations become more and more difficult over vast geographical areas. Immediately in the greeting of Bishop Pardy is Bishop Chang's plea for forgiveness after failing to fulfill the duties of filial piety, highlighting the importance of respecting one's elder and observing the familial bond for the people of Korean descent. This situation is further exacerbated when the parish reflects the household. As with most Asian societies, the church literally represents God's family, a household on earth, more so than perhaps anywhere else. Thus, bishops and priests enjoy the place of honor as the head of this particular household. With such authority and honor placed on the clergy, the failure to uphold the observance of filial piety becomes even more serious. The failure to acknowledge and include Bishop Pardy in the daily consciousness in the lives of Korean Catholics in the Diocese of Cheongju resembles a grave transgression (more so in the Confucian sense than in Catholicism, although the two can be easily identified with

---

[2] See the appendix for a complete translation of Bishop Gabriel Chang's homily marking the transfer of Bishop James Pardy's remains.

each other), but more importantly further exemplifies the way Koreans remember or fail to remember their past.

As previously mentioned, without some pinnacle of success where there are no rivals, as in the case of St. Andrew Kim, it becomes nearly impossible for Koreans to embrace their past, especially when it is filled with such painful memories. For the people of the Cheongju diocese, it was the recovery from the devastation of war even almost a decade later and the poverty surrounding them when Bishop Pardy shepherded their spiritual lives. Because of impoverished conditions of the times and the personal nature of *han* within every Korean, walking with past memories only intensified the shame and pain associated with personal struggles without any hopeful signs except the future. Thus, the hope in releasing one's *han* is seen only in future possibilities and not in the past. The drive for success in education, social status, wealth, and even in church growth among Koreans became intensified within an entire generation. Luckily, the Catholic Church in Korea has enjoyed much success in various forms to now begin embracing even the difficult moments of their past. Unfortunately, the Korean immigrant church has not been afforded such luxuries.

Once milestones are attained in church and society, occasions such as the one in the Diocese of Cheongju to recall and honor certain memories of the past become acceptable. In particular, those who reached the pinnacle of their field, becoming exemplars without any equal, are easily embraced. In the Diocese of Cheongju, the success of Catholicism is now intricately linked with Bishop Pardy as the first episcopal leader of that region. With every figure upheld in church or society, hundreds and even thousands go unnoticed. There are, however, essential pieces for such figures to rise to the forefront. On the one hand, the remembrance of Bishop Pardy is long overdue, as reflected in Bishop Chang's homily. On the other hand, this occasion escapes us without pausing for a moment in honoring the faithful who laid the foundations of the Catholic Church in Cheongju but do not necessarily receive the same acclaim. Forgiveness for the inability to fulfill our duties and responsibilities of filial piety must be asked of them as well.

The lesson for all Catholics of Korean descent is that as difficult as it may be to embrace the past, it is a necessary step forward, especially when carrying our cultural crosses. When the past is not properly carried throughout every stage of our lives, people are forgotten, events become lost, and a people without proper identity and self-confidence emerge. Thus, the carrying of our cultural cross is painful, but in the end it allows us to avoid the unpleasant realizations of people, places, and events forgotten, as in the case of Bishop Pardy.

Just as Simon of Cyrene helped Jesus carry the cross, our cultural crosses cannot be carried alone. Rather, we must walk with one another. Simon, most likely, did not volunteer to carry Jesus' cross but rather was thrown into this task because of the situation. Perhaps he was the closest one around, maybe he appeared the strongest or most sympathetic, or maybe he simply made eye contact, commissioning himself into the service of the Lord. In any case, Simon left a different man that day after carrying the cross. How could a person not be changed after witnessing the brutality against another human being? How could a person not question his religion, society, and people after experiencing the crucifixion on the side of the accused innocent? Whatever the reasons for Simon being chosen to carry the cross, he left Golgotha a different man. Carrying our cultural crosses will also change the way we deal with our innermost reality, especially in dealing with *han*.

The Stations of the Cross provide another vital lesson for Catholics of Korean descent. The Way of the Cross as remembered in our faith tradition recounts Jesus falling three times. The question why the church remembered this event on three different occasions must be raised. Was the fall recounted in this manner since it was the actual snapshot of each moment? Perhaps a more plausible answer would be that the fall of Jesus was recounted three times to indicate an ongoing nature of the Way of the Cross. In order to pick up the cross and walk this particular path, it meant that ongoing falls, ongoing stumbles, and ongoing failures would always be part of the journey. This way was ordained by the Lord, for it was the chosen path. It is also a reflection of the way our lives will be lived out as we continually fall, stumble, and fail. However, in this falling, stumbling, and failing, we become holy since this is the way of the cross. We reach the pinnacles of our faith, not in our own images of reaching new heights, especially in the case of Korean Americans and Koreans alike in the hopes of releasing their *han*. Rather, the pinnacle that Christ reveals to us is reached in the gospel sense contrary to the things of this world, as we continue to pick ourselves up after every fall.

The Korean American Promise

As unfamiliar, uncomfortable, and unpleasant a life on the margins may be, Korean American Catholics are still in a privileged place to witness how the context of the immigrant experience positively affects the transmission and reception of the lived faith experience. In particular, how departure, displacement, and resettlement can re-create one's history in light of salvation history. As people of a Korean descent living as an immigrant or offspring of one, Korean American Catholics have a diverse context whereby Scripture and traditions are able to come more fully alive. Being an immigrant, ethnic minority and a religious minority, since most Korean Americans are Protestants, Korean American Catholics have much work in comprehending their unique situation as a blessing. Without proper reflection, the passing on of the faith to the next generation in its Korean context lived out by the initial immigrant group becomes foreign. Without the lived faith experience that includes experiences of departure, displacement, and resettlement resonating with the subsequent generation, the next generation of Korean American Catholics will view their parents' faith as antiquated and irrelevant in the context of their lives. Even worse, their situation in life never reaches the promise they are called to bring forth. The Korean American promise is that by living in two different worlds, caught in between two languages and customs, arises a way of incorporating the best of both worlds. By doing so, Korean Americans can show those living in the diaspora as well as in their homeland that the release of *han* is achieved not through the traditional categories Koreans strive for but in the reimaging of their lives where the deficiencies and shortcomings are humbly accepted and embraced in making up their humanity. By doing so, *han* continues in the people of Korean descent but no longer has the same destructive controls of the past.

Being descendants of a Korean Catholic heritage means that Korean Americans have inherited a rich faith tradition like no other. As modern-day recipients of "Koreanized" Catholicism, Korean American Catholics must learn from the lessons of salvation history, especially as it has been lived out in the Korean peninsula. The history of Catholicism in Korea has echoed the lived tradition of Catholicism in general. Since the first believers of the Way, Catholics have endured much persecution. However, it was not just persecution that allowed the faith to grow in vibrant ways. Rather, it was the outward profession of faith as Catholics spoke out against injustices on behalf of others and led social and political reforms even at the expense of their own lives during moments of Christian persecution. The history of Christianity is a vivid reminder of this reality.

In the nineteenth century when Catholicism was gaining a foothold on the Korean peninsula, the people who professed such a belief were persecuted for their seemingly contradictory lifestyle to the long-standing Confucian society. The unwillingness to renounce their newly found faith cost many their lives. The active laity willing to lay down their lives became role models for Catholics to live out their lives in public even under the most difficult circumstances. In the beginning of the twentieth century, the Catholic Church in Korea took a different position in all social and political situations, leaving the church out of worldly affairs. This lack of social and political engagement is not just one of many reasons why the Protestant faith immerged in Korea but perhaps the primary one. History at the turn of the century reveals that the inward focus of the Catholic Church led to relative calm in their ecclesial existence but this focus did not endear themselves to the masses who sought independence from Japanese colonialism. Protestants were at the forefront in social and political causes as they resisted Japanese occupation, built hospitals with the aid of U.S. missionaries, and constructed schools to continue the Confucian heritage that stressed the importance of education.

Once the Catholic Church escaped persecution and social responsibility, the church became a nonfactor in the lives of Koreans. The modest growth of new Catholics in the first half of the twentieth century is dwarfed by the numbers who embraced the Protestant faith, a reminder that a church separated from the world becomes forgotten. Soon after WWII and the civil war, the Korean Catholic Church returned to its roots to lead the impoverished people back to spiritual and social health. Catholics led by the growing indigenous clergy became involved in all aspects of society. By building hospitals, schools, and other social agencies, the Catholic Church created a bridge into the daily lives of the masses and became relevant once again. With increased participation in social and political concerns, Catholicism was embraced widely in society as membership rapidly increased. A priest from Korea recently told me that it is hard to rival the social status of Catholic clergy in modern-day society. Whether Catholics or Protestants, both churches grew under persecution and difficult moments when they actively engaged the people in their social concerns. Both denominations were embraced by the masses when hospitals, schools, and other social structures bearing their names were created. These physical edifices were symbolic of the commitment the churches were making on behalf of society, regardless of denominational affiliation.

Immigrants of Korean and Catholic descent in the U.S. have not fully understood this historical lesson. As with most immigrants, the creation of an ethnic enclave provides certain protection living in a foreign land where the interaction with mainstream or other minority groups does not easily occur. Korean immigrants who came to the U.S. after immigration standards were lessened in 1965 did so without many resources, skills, or English-language proficiency. Korean immigrants of this generation were preoccupied in making ends meet in order to survive. This survival-mode mentality became a central characteristic within the ethnic enclave. Thoughts of social contributions or involvement outside the family or Korean community are virtually nonexistent in this immigrant group. The survival-mode mentality fueled the immigrants' will as they labored long hours in difficult working conditions. This mentality not only served for self-preservation of the individual in the resettlement process but also provided for the future welfare of their children.

Church building was one way immigrants of recent memory were able to contribute and take ownership in a new land. With limited resources while surviving in a new country, Korean immigrants gave back very little to society outside their immediate circles. Thus, the construction of a church represents hope—a hope that their religious and cultural heritage would continue outside of Korea. By contributing to a church-building campaign, Korean immigrants feel "safe" in their financial giving since they know how their contributions will be used. The limited family resources during the survival-mode period required such securities. In addition, the construction of their own religious house allowed this immigrant generation to take some form of ownership in the U.S., which at times seemed so foreign and elusive to them. A religious edifice was a visible symbol, much like their homes and businesses, that they had ownership and a place of refuge in an unfamiliar society. Outside of "secure-giving" campaigns where funds are fully accounted for, with an understood common purpose and lasting ownership in the project, Koreans are rarely compelled to give if there are no returns to their well-being due to their survival-mode mentality. The next generation of Korean Americans has yet to discover their place in church and society as reflected in the unwillingness and inability to contribute financially, thereby making a personal commitment.

The immigration experience places Korean American Catholics out of touch with social concerns. Often, societal problems are seen as a result of negative American culture and values, thus isolating Korean Americans further into their ethnic communities. Although physical persecution does not necessarily exist in a country touting religious freedom as one of its foundations for society, Korean Americans still face a multitude of other forms of discrimination. By no means are these moments of injustice equivalent to past martyrdoms suffered in the early church. They are only recounted here to show the emotional pressures further keeping the Korean people within their ethnic groups. The history of Korean Christianity illustrates the need for social engagement under difficult public encounters rather than a withdrawal. Only by engaging difficult circumstances in the public forum did Christianity flourish by attracting new members and passing on a faith that was relevant to people's lives. The faith floundered when Christian communities retreated into themselves, fearing the world around them and seeking a false sense of security within a familiar but isolated world.

Likewise, unless Korean American Catholics find a way to engage society by discovering their contribution, the relevancy of the Catholic faith within this ethnic setting will become less and less. Already we are witnessing the difficulties of passing on Catholic and Korean traditions because of the isolated world of the initial immigrant groups in their current ecclesial setting. Whereas, the older generation had at least their homes, businesses, and church that they financially supported, giving them a sense of ownership and belonging, the next generation typically has the sense neither of social responsibility nor of calling the U.S. their true home. The next generation must not only prosper in their education and careers as provided for by their parents' struggles but, more importantly, prosper in making a contribution to the larger society, going beyond religious and ethnic boundaries. Only by contributing to society can Korean Americans take ownership and create a space of belonging in a multicultural environment. In addition, the gospel imperative is to care for all as our brothers and sisters, regardless of religious and ethnic differences. To truly be Korean, American, and Catholic requires a movement beyond the comforts of the world the immigrant groups created in their survival-mode mentality and to engage society with the richness of being Korean American Catholics.

The lack of social engagement is almost never addressed in Korean American Catholic circles. Many attribute the lack of interest in the faith of their parents largely due to the ignorance of the next generation. Since Koreans highly stress education, they will simply instruct others to study more intensely when things do not work out. Often, the lack of catechetical and scriptural knowledge is the excuse made as to why the younger generation fails to take the Catholic faith seriously. However, the complicated and complex reality of immigrants and the next generation, especially in passing on cultural and religious values, cannot simply be explained by a lack of knowledge. Greater dynamics are at play where knowledge must be reconciled with the lived reality of Korean Americans.

Finding a Voice

As stated in the previous chapters, Korean American Catholics are facing tremendous pressures by being compared to others. Facing pressures from the Catholic Church in Korea with its unprecedented growth, the hard work and dedication of the immigrant generation, the Christian majority Korean American Protestants, and the dominant English-speaking Catholics, Korean American Catholics must now more than ever find their voice. Without a voice, Korean American Catholics will have a difficult time looking forward with hope, for the past has yet to be reconciled. At risk is both their religious and cultural heritage. Although the cultural heritage can continue in the lives of the next generation in other forms and through other structures, the immigrant experience of their families is a key component to maintaining their ethnic and religious identity. The context of departure, displacement, and resettlement is constitutive for a Korean American identity as well as a Catholic identity based on one's ethnicity. Thus, it is pertinent that Korean American Catholics find a voice for themselves and future generations. This task cannot be done by others but through a proper reflection upon the received religious and cultural traditions within the lived experience of immigration. The voice arising from this reflection will serve Korean American Catholics in many ways; in particular, it will have a specific twofold purpose.

The first purpose in finding a Korean American Catholic voice is to express the needs which are currently being overlooked and overshadowed in the immigrant church model. The next generation of Korean American Catholics must voice their needs in order to have the church respond to them regardless of their population size. One criteria of holiness for a faith community is how well they care for the least among them. The twenty-fifth chapter of Matthew reminds us that at the last judgment when the sheep are separated from the goats, the criteria of that separation will be based on our actions to those who are the least among us. In verses 40 and 45, twice Jesus reminds us: "Amen, I say to you, whatever you did for one of these least brothers of mine, you did for me" (NAB).

Future generations needing the church's spiritual and cultural foundations will be at a loss without such interaction and dialogue. The voice of the next generation must not fall on deaf ears but on the ears of Korean priests and sisters, initial and recent immigrants, and themselves. Too often, pastors and religious sisters from Korea come with a temporary missioner mind-set since their assignments are for four years. In addition, the lack of desire to learn the English language and American culture compounds the situation, whereby the next generation rarely gets the pastoral care they need. Without hearing from the next generation, Korean-speaking pastors, religious sisters, and the initial immigrant parent group will continue to model the immigrant church in the manner they are familiar and comfortable with back home. Thus, they will continue to minister solely to the immigrant group unless the next generation becomes a presence in the church and begins to voice their concerns. Part of the difficulty in voicing the needs of Korean Americans is that this generation does not have the adequate skill sets and resources to identify their spiritual and cultural needs as well as the ability to voice given their background of growing up in a Korean household and church.

This inability or lack of skills to engage their social and religious situation in a coherent manner is not simply an issue arising from the immigrant experience. Rather, the aversion to directly addressing one's current reality can be traced in Korean Christianity. This is not to say that Korean Americans are genetically disposed to a certain behavior but rather that the challenges are much greater since Koreans in general have had a long history of difficulties in this regard. The mind-set that Korean Americans must overcome in naming and claiming their religious and cultural identity goes beyond denominational affiliation as it is a perspective whereby Koreans look to the future almost at the risk of letting go of the present. Instead of addressing their reality, Koreans have a tendency to look to the otherworldly, thereby almost disregarding their current situation.

From the beginning of Christianity in Korea, looking beyond this world mentality was ingrained in the first believers who needed this comfort as they faced immense poverty and persecution.

> Korean Catholics during the persecution period showed more interest in life after death than in life before death . . . [A] reason for this abstemiousness was so that Catholics could find the spiritual strength they needed to survive the poverty caused by maintaining their faith. Catholic valorization of the soul over the body and the life in the later world over that of this world is articulated in the phrase *saju kuryŏng* (serving the Lord and saving souls). In response to continuing persecution by the government, Catholics embraced the suffering of this world while simultaneously working toward the salvation of their souls in heaven. Reminding each other of *saju kuryŏng*, they aspired to maintain their faith and be martyred. Martyrdom was regarded as an honor and heaven as one's true home.[3]

---

[3] Inshil Choe Yoon, "Martyrdom and Social Activism: The Korean Practice of Catholicism," in *Religions of Korea in Practice*, ed. Robert Buswell (Princeton, NJ: Princeton University Press, 2007), 358.

In almost a similar manner, Korean immigrants have embraced the hardships of departure, displacement, and resettlement unquestioned in lieu of the next generation's success and their eternal reward. Much of the same motivation for enduring persecution of the early Korean Catholics still operates as the motivation for the immigrant generation.

The second purpose in finding their voice for the next generation stems from their responsibilities to the future generations of Korean American Catholics. Being in a position where some Korean American Catholics are able to bridge their parents' world as well as mainstream society, the next generation must begin asking questions so that answers may be sought out now and in the future. "But we must not forget that those who change the course of history are usually these who pose a new set of questions rather than those who offer solutions."[4] Questions, not answers, are what transform hearts and minds.

The immigrant mind-set is broadened to include the needs outside their own by properly posing the questions reflecting the status of their lives. And our hearts are transformed as we become compassionate to those yet to come as well as those who are caught in between two realities by voicing questions pertaining not only to them but perhaps to future generations. The questions we ask will give the next generation a chance to clarify their identity, gain confidence, and hope in the church, making their spiritual home relevant as they navigate the world with similar issues.

[4] Gustavo Gutiérrez, introduction to *Between Honesty and Hope: Documents from and about the Church in Latin America: Issued at Lima by the Peruvian Bishops' Commission for Social Action*, ed. Peruvian Bishops' Commission for Social Action, trans. John Drury (Maryknoll, NY: Orbis, 1970), xxiii.

Appendix

Sermon Preached at the Mass on November 30, 2011, Marking the Transfer of Bishop James Pardy's Remains

1. We have gathered here today to offer Mass and to mark the transfer of the remains of our first bishop, James V. Pardy. I am grateful to all the faithful, the sisters, and the priests who have come here today despite the winter rain.

2. Last evening at seven o'clock, when we welcomed Bishop Pardy and received his remains at the former chancery office, now the Catholic Youth Center, where for eleven years from 1958 to 1969 he carried out his work as the first bishop of the diocese, my first words of greeting to him were, "Thank you, Bishop."

   Last night, thirty-five years after leaving Korea in 1976 [he retired as ordinary of the diocese in 1969 and spent the next seven years at Sacred Heart Home for the Aged, now the site of the bishop's residence and the chancery office], Bishop Pardy returned to his flock as a handful of ashes [as ashes in a small urn] and I had one more word of greeting, "We are truly sorry. Please forgive us."

3. The Maryknoll Fathers and Brothers first received the mandate to evangelize North Chungcheong Province in 1953. At that time Bishop Pardy became the Vicar Forane for three years, and then for another eleven years, from 1958 until 1969, the year of his retirement, he was the diocesan bishop. There was nothing here, and he had to lay the foundation and formulate a system for the diocese.

   Taking responsibility for the diocese was evangelization. The church is in this world and Jesus founded his church to continue the work

111

of redemption until the end of the world. For the work of redemption, however, two things are required. First, there must be a church building, the school of salvation, where the Gospel can be preached. Secondly, there must be priests to preach the Gospel continuously and to offer Mass and administer the sacraments.

When Bishop Pardy was appointed as the first Vicar Forane in 1953, there were five churches and eight thousand Catholics in North Chungcheong Province. There was not a single Korean priest. But when Bishop Pardy retired in 1969 in the Province (including Checheon and Tan Yang), there were twenty-five parishes, 272 mission stations, 106 chapels, and 51,931 Catholics. Moreover, there were six Korean priests and many seminarians.

To provide a base and strategic position for evangelization, Bishop Pardy during his time in office prepared land for churches and mission stations and constructed twenty churches. Moreover, in order that local communities might be the centers of evangelization he constructed 106 mission stations. For spreading the Gospel in North Chungcheong Province truly Bishop Pardy was a strategist and a visionary, leaving churches and mission stations in every large area down to the myons. He was the foundation of evangelization and provided infrastructure. We are most grateful for this.

Bishop Pardy worked hard to develop vocations and to nurture priests. In every parish he organized the CYO for Catholic youth. In every parish he arranged to have basketball and volleyball courts where young people could meet. In every parish he provided foreign books and spiritual reading material as a way to promote vocations. Through the cultivating of Korean priests in the Chungbuk area he positively arranged pivotal points for evangelization. He developed priests as the most important element for evangelizing. While playing on the parish sports fields and while reading books in the parish libraries, the faith of young people was nurtured, and with Bishop Pardy's letter of recommendation they entered the minor seminary and in time became priests. In 1953, when the Maryknoll Fathers and Brothers received the mandate to evangelize North Chungcheong Province, the country had been ravaged by the Korean War, and North Chungcheong Province had especially fallen behind, and there were many living in the shadow of poverty and hopelessness. Bishop Pardy enthusiastically developed relief work and gave to the many starving people in Chungbuk something to eat and to those without clothing something to wear. Furthermore, through medical work, especially at the Maryknoll clinic in Chung Pyeong and in the stations for free medicine in Ok Cheon and Poun, countless patients were relieved of their pain and were led back to life. Also in parishes, credit unions were founded, and in rural areas, animal cooperatives were developed. Through the operation of these programs, poor people and farmers were given hope.

On this kind of foundation, the Cheongju diocese has flourished so that the people living in this area today say that among the various religions the Catholic Church is number one for goodness and truthfulness, Catholics are 11 percent of the population and among the sixteen dioceses this diocese ranks third in its percentage of Catholics. We sincerely thank you for this, Bishop Pardy.

4. Last night at seven o'clock, thirty-five years after leaving Korea [after he left the diocese he returned to the U.S., where after much suffering he died in a nursing home from Lou Gehrig's disease], Bishop Pardy returned to his flock in a small urn and I greeted him with one more word, "forgive us."

The saying goes, "Engrave an enemy in stone and engrave a benefactor in water." We have forgotten you completely, Bishop, and have gone on with our lives. We have forgotten your generosity and blessings and have gone on with our lives. No one went to see the forgotten bishop after his retirement; no one phoned you, nor did we send you a Christmas card. No one was there to watch at your death bed. For twenty-eight years after your death, no one visited your grave, and this is no exaggeration.

They say that the greatest pain and sadness for parents is to be cast out by their children. They say that the greatest pain and sadness for parents, the greatest anger and despair that they can feel, is to be forgotten by the children they raised with love, the offspring they put their hope in, to live totally estranged.

At this time let us all bend our knees and beg together that the bishop who gave us blessings like water during his long life will forgive us for our lack of filial piety.

5. As a flock, even though it is late, we have become more sensitive. In observing the fifty years since the establishment of the diocese we have sorted out and reflected on the events of the half century and we have

been led to remember first of all our bishop. We have come to know his goodness and generosity. Even though it is very late, by the grace of God, in this meaningful year marking the one-hundredth anniversary of the founding of Maryknoll, we are happy that we are able to bury the bishop here in the priests' section of St. Joseph Cemetery among the waiting flock he shepherded.

For a long time we forgot Bishop Pardy, but God never forgot all his goodness. Today is truly a day that God has made. After the bishop left the diocese as if in the fulfillment of a dream, God in a timely way saw to the construction of the Catholic Youth Center on the site of the former bishop's residence and chancery office. God mysteriously saw to all of this. A few days ago on November 26 we had the blessing of the Center and then last night, November 29, God prepared it so that the bishop's remains were received in the new Center.

Then God prepared things so that, as the bishop wished, he was able to be buried with his flock in the 150,000 pyong St. Joseph Cemetery that the bishop himself had bought. In a timely fashion the hill has been cut away, the road was widened, and a church and dining room were prepared. So it was also prepared that today the dining room is being used for the first time.

As we offer this Mass, let us promise that we will not forget our first bishop who has been buried close by, and let us promise that whenever we come to the cemetery we will visit his grave.

Bibliography

Baker, Don. *Korean Spirituality*. Honolulu: University of Hawaii Press, 2008.

Burns, Jeffrey M., Ellen Skerrett, and Joseph M. White. *Keeping Faith: European and Asian Catholic Immigrants*. Maryknoll, NY: Orbis Books, 2000.

Buswell, Robert, ed. *Religions of Korea in Practice*. Princeton, NJ: Princeton University Press, 2007.

Cha, Peter T. *The Role of a Korean-American Church in the Construction of Ethnic Identities among Second-Generation Korean Americans*. Ph.D. diss., Northwestern University, Evanston, IL, 2002.

Chae, Mark H., and Pamela F. Foley. "Relationships of Ethnic Identity, Acculturation, and Psychological Well-Being among Chinese, Japanese, and Korean Americans." *Journal of Counseling and Development* 88 (2010): 466–76.

Chai, Karen J. "Competing for the Second Generation: English-Language Ministry at a Korean Protestant Church." In *Gatherings in Diaspora: Religious and the New Immigration*, edited by R. Stephan Warner and Judith G. Wittner, 295–332. Philadelphia: Temple University Press, 1998.

Cho, Grace. *Haunting the Korean Diaspora: Shame, Secrecy, and the Forgotten War*. Minneapolis: University of Minnesota Press, 2008.

Choi, Chungmoo. "The Discourse of Decolonization and Popular Memory: South Korea." *Positions: East Asia Cultures Critique* 1, no. 1 (1993): 77–102.

Choi, Hee An. *Korean Women and God: Experiencing God in a Multi-religious Colonial Context*. Maryknoll, NY: Orbis Books, 2005.

Choi, Hyaeweol. "A New Moral Order: Gender Equality in Korean Christianity." In *Religions of Korea in Practice*, edited by Robert Buswell, 409–20. Princeton, NJ: Princeton University Press, 2007.

Choi, Jai-Keun. *The Origin of the Roman Catholic Church in Korea: An Examination of Popular and Governmental Responses to Catholic Missions in the Late Choson Dynasty*. Seoul, Korea: Hermit Kingdom Press, 2006.

Choy, Bong Youn. *Koreans in America*. Chicago: Nelson-Hall, 1979.

Chu, Seo-Young. "Science Fiction and Postmemory of Han in Contemporary Korean American Literature." *MELUS* 33, no. 4 (2008): 97–121.

Chung, Angie Y. *Legacies of Struggle: Conflict and Cooperation in Korean American Politics*. Stanford: Stanford University Press, 2007.

Chung, Chai-Sik. "Confucian Tradition and Values: Implications for Conflict in Modern Korea." In *Religions in Korea: Beliefs and Cultural Values*, edited by Earl H. Phillips and Eui-Young Yu, 99–116. Los Angeles: Center for Korean-American and Korean Studies, 1982.

Curry, Thomas J. "A Korean Catholic Experience: St. Philip Neri Parish in the Archdiocese of Boston." *U.S. Catholic Historian* 18, no. 1 (2000): 111–25.

Dries, Angelyn. "Korean Catholics in the United States." *U.S. Catholic Historian* 18, no. 1 (2000): 99–110.

Foner, Nancy. "Introduction: Intergenerational Relations in Immigrant Families." In *Across Generations: Immigrants Families in America*, edited by Nancy Foner, 1–20. New York: New York University Press, 2009.

———, ed. *Across Generations: Immigrants Families in America*. New York: New York University Press, 2009.

Gi-bong, Kim. "The Legacy of Cho Seung-hui: America's Lesson to Koreans." *Korea JoongAng Daily*, April 25, 2007. Accessed August 24, 2011. http://watchingamerica.com/joongangdaily000036.shtml.

Grayson, James Huntley. "The Grieving Rite: A Protestant Response to Confucian Ancestral Rituals." In *Religions of Korea in Practice*, edited by Robert Buswell, 434–45. Princeton, NJ: Princeton University Press, 2007.

———. *Korea: A Religious History*. London: RoutledgeCurzon, 2002.

Gutiérrez, Gustavo. Introduction to *Between Honesty and Hope: Documents from and about the Church in Latin America: Issued at Lima by the Peruvian Bishops' Commission for Social Action*, edited by Peruvian Bishops' Commission for Social Action, translated by John Drury, xii–xxiv. Maryknoll, NY: Orbis, 1970.

Han, Jin, and Cameron Lee. "Ministry Demand and Stress among Korean American Pastors: A Brief Report." *Pastoral Psychology* 52, no. 6 (2004): 473–78.

Hoover, Brett. "The Shared Parish." *American Catholic Studies Newsletter* 37, no. 2 (2010): 1, 7–10.

Houchins, Lee, and Chang-su Houchins. "The Korean Experience in America, 1903–1924." *Pacific Historical Review* 43, no. 4 (1974): 548–75.

Hovey, Joseph, Sheena Kim, and Laura Seligman. "The Influences of Cultural Values, Ethnic Identity, and Language Use on the Mental Health of Korean American College Students." *The Journal of Psychology* 140, no. 5 (2006): 499–511.

Hurh, Won Moo, and Kwang Chung Kim. *Korean Immigrants in America: A Structural Analysis of Ethnic Confinement and Adhesive Adaptation*. Cranbury, NJ: Associated University Presses, 1984.

Jo, Moon H. *Korean Immigrants and the Challenge of Adjustment.* Westport, CT: Greenwood Press, 1999.

Kelly, Kevin R., Ae-Jung Chang Gunsalus, and Robert Gunsalus. "Social Cognitive Predictors of the Career Goals of Korean American Students." *The Career Development Quarterly* 58 (2009): 14–28.

Kendall, Laurel. *The Life and Hard Times of a Korean Shaman: Of Tales and the Telling of Tales.* Honolulu: University of Hawaii Press, 1988.

———. *Shamans, Housewives, and Other Restless Spirits: Women in Korean Ritual Life.* Honolulu: University of Hawaii Press, 1985.

Kim, Chan-Hie. "Christianity and the Modernization of Korea." In *Religions in Korea: Beliefs and Cultural Values,* edited by Earl H. Phillips and Eui-Young Yu, 117–27. Los Angeles: Center for Korean-American and Korean Studies, 1982.

Kim, Elaine H. "Home Is Where the Han Is: A Korean American Perspective on the Los Angeles Upheavels." In *Reading Rodney King: Reading Urban Uprising,* edited by Robert Gooding-Williams, 215–35. New York: Routledge, 1993.

Kim, Eunjung. "Psychological Adjustment in Young Korean American Adolescents and Parental Warmth." *Journal of Child and Adolescent Psychiatric Nursing* 21, no. 4 (2008): 195–201.

Kim, Eunjung, and Seth Wolpin. "The Korean American Family: Adolescents Versus Parents Acculturation to American Culture." *Journal of Cultural Diversity* 15, no. 3 (2008): 108–16.

Kim, Hyung-chan, and Wayne Patterson, eds. *The Koreans in America 1882–1974: A Chronology and Fact Book.* Dobbs Ferry, NY: Oceana Publication, 1974.

Kim, Joseph Chang-mun, and John Jae-sun Chung, eds. *Catholic Korea: Yesterday and Today.* Seoul, Korea: Catholic Korea, 1964.

Kim, Matthew. "Possible Selves: A Homiletic for Second Generation Korean American Churches." *Homiletic* 32, no. 1 (2007): 1–17.

Kim, Min-Jung. "Moments of Danger in the (Dis)continuous Relation of Korean Nationalism and Korean American Nationalism." *Positions* 5, no. 2 (1997): 357–89.

Kim, Sharon. *A Faith of Our Own: Second-Generation Spirituality in Korean American Churches.* Piscataway, NJ: Rutgers University Press, 2010.

———. "Shifting Boundaries within Second-Generation Korean American Churches." *Sociology of Religion* 71, no. 1 (2010): 98–122.

Klein, Kerwin Lee. "In Search of Narrative Mastery: Postmodernism and the People without History." *History and Theory* 34, no. 4 (1995): 275–98.

Koo, Mark C. *Conversion Experience in Korea: Gospel Insights of Forgiveness within the HAN Culture.* Ph.D. diss., Graduate Theological Union Berkeley, CA, 2001.

Lee, Hwain C. *Confucius, Christ and Co-Partnership: Competing Liturgies for the Soul of Korean American Women.* Lanham, MD: University Press of America, 1993.

Lee, Jennifer, Esther Chang, and Lisa Miller. "Ethnic-Religious Status and Identity Formation: A Qualitative Study of Korean American Christian Youth." *The Journal of Youth Ministry* 5, no. 1 (2006): 9–40.

Lee, Samuel. "Navigating between Cultures: A New Paradigm for Korean American Cultural Identification." *Pastoral Psychology* 54, no. 4 (2006): 289–311.

Lee, Sung-Ae. "Re-visioning Gendered Folktales in Novels by Mia Yun and Nora Okja Keller." *Asian Ethnology* 68, no. 1 (2009): 131–50.

Lee, Timothy S. "Conversion Narratives in Korean Evangelicalism." In *Religions of Korea in Practice*, edited by Robert Buswell, 393–408. Princeton, NJ: Princeton University Press, 2007.

———. "Indigenized Devotional Practices in Korean Evangelicalism." In *Religions of Korea in Practice*, edited by Robert Buswell, 421–33. Princeton, NJ: Princeton University Press, 2007.

Min, Anselm Kyongsuk. "Korean American Catholic Communities." In *Religion and Spirituality in Korean America*, edited by David Yoon and Ruth Chung, 21–39. Champaign: University of Illinois Press, 2008.

Min, Pyong Gap. *Preserving Ethnicity through Religion in America: Korean Protestants and Indian Hindus across Generations.* New York: New York University Press, 2010.

Min, Pyong Gap, and Dae Young Kim. "Intergenerational Transmission of Religion and Culture: Korean Protestants in the U.S." *Sociology of Religion* 66, no. 3 (2005): 263–82.

Oh, Angela E. "An Issue of Time and Place: The Truth behind Korean Americans' Connection to the 1992 Los Angeles Riots." *Harvard Journal of Asian American Policy Review* 19 (2010): 39–48.

Oum, Young Rae. "Authenticity and Representation: Cuisines and Identities in Korean-American Diaspora." *Postcolonial Studies* 8, no. 1 (2005): 109–25.

Park, Andrew Sung. "The Formation of Multicultural Religious Identity within Persons in Korean-American Experience." *The Journal of Pastoral Theology* 13, no. 2 (2003): 34–50.

———. *From Hurt to Healing: A Theology of the Wounded.* Nashville, TN: Abingdon Press, 2004.

———. *The Wounded Heart of God: The Asian Concept of Han and the Christian Doctrine of Sin.* Nashville, TN: Abingdon Press, 1993.

Park, Kil Jae. "Yellow on White Background: Korean American Youth Ministry and the Challenge of Constructing Korean American Identity." *The Journal of Youth Ministry* 4, no. 1 (2005): 23–36.

Phan, Peter. "'Presence and Prominence in the Lord's House': Asians and Pacific People in the American Catholic Church." In *Many Faces, One Church: Cultural Diversity and the American Catholic Experience*, edited by Peter Phan, 99–116. New York: Sheed & Ward, 2004.

Phillips, Earl H., and Eui-Young Yu, eds. *Religions in Korea: Beliefs and Cultural Values*. Los Angeles: Center for Korean-American and Korean Studies, 1982.

Rausch, Franklin, and Don Baker. "Catholic Rites and Liturgy." In *Religions of Korea in Practice*, edited by Robert Buswell, 376–92. Princeton, NJ: Princeton University Press, 2007.

Takaki, Ronald. *Strangers from a Different Shore*. New York: Penguin Books, 1989.

USCCB. "Asian and Pacific Presence: Harmony in Faith." *United States Conference of Catholic Bishops, Inc.* 2001. Accessed February 20, 2012. http://usccb .org/issues-and-action/cultural-diversity/asian-pacific-islander/resources /bishops-statement-asian-pacific-island.cfm.

———. *A Catholic Response to the Asian Presence*. Washington, D.C.: National Catholic Educational Association, 1990.

———. "Welcoming the Stranger among Us: Unity in Diversity." United States Conference of Catholic Bishops, Inc., 2000. Accessed February 20, 2012. http://usccb.org/issues-and-action/cultural-diversity/pastoral-care -of-migrants-refugees-and-travelers/resources/welcoming-the-stranger -among-us-unity-in-diversity.cfm.

Warner, R. Stephen. "Korean Americans Reshape Their Churches." *Christian Century* (2007): 30–32.

Warner, R. Stephan, and Judith G. Wittner, eds. *Gatherings in Diaspora: Religious Communities and the New Immigration*. Philadelphia: Temple University Press, 1998.

Yoon, David, and Ruth Chung. *Religion and Spirituality in Korean America*. Champaign: University of Illinois Press, 2008.

Yoon, Inshil Choe. "Martyrdom and Social Activism: The Korean Practice of Catholicism." In *Religions of Korea in Practice*, edited by Robert Buswell, 355–75. Princeton, NJ: Princeton University Press, 2007.

Simon C. Kim is assistant professor of theology and coordinator of the Catholic Intellectual Tradition program at Our Lady of Holy Cross College in New Orleans, Louisiana. He earned a PhD in theology from The Catholic University of America in 2011, specializing in theology in cross-cultural contexts. He works extensively with Korean American communities and offers conferences, workshops, and retreats across the country on Korean American pastoral ministry.